VERONICA FORREST-THOMSON
AND
LANGUAGE POETRY

Miles Thomson

VERONICA FORREST-THOMSON

VERONICA FORREST-THOMSON AND LANGUAGE POETRY

ALISON MARK

Northcote House
in association with the
British Council

First published in 2001 by Northcote House Publishers Ltd, Horndon, Tavistock, Devon, PL19 9NQ, United Kingdom.
Tel: +44 (01822) 810066 Fax: +44 (01822) 810034.

British Library Cataloguing-in-Publication Data
A catalogue record for this book is available from the British Library

ISBN 0-7463-0912-0
Typeset by PDQ Typesetting, Newcastle-under-Lyme
Printed and bound in the United Kingdom by
The Baskerville Press Ltd, Salisbury, Wiltshire, SP2 7QB

For David,
and in memory of my beloved Father

Contents

Acknowledgements

I wish to thank everyone who made this book possible: Isobel Armstrong, who commissioned it and first introduced me to Forrest-Thomson's work; Carol Watts, who supervised my doctoral work on Forrest-Thomson; and all the poets and writers, friends and acquaintances, academics and enthusiasts, at conferences, readings, and other places who have contributed to my love for and knowledge of this subject, especially Charles Bernstein, Helen Carr, Alan Golding, Robert Hampson, Jane Harrison, Carla Harryman, Lyn Hejinian, Susan Howe, Romana Huk, Karen MacCormack, Steve McCaffery, Brian McHale, Peter Middleton, Wendy Mulford, Maggie O'Sullivan, Bob Perelman, Marjorie Perloff, Suzanne Raitt, Deryn Rees-Jones, Denise Riley, Robert Sheppard, Hazel Smith, David Turnbull, Geoff Ward, and Barrett Watten. Naturally, the responsibility for any omissions or errors is my own. Particular thanks are due to Jonathan Culler, Forrest-Thomson's literary executor, for his unfailing kindness and generosity with archival material, and for his helpful comments on the final draft. Thanks also to Anthony Barnett, editor of the invaluable *Collected Poems and Translations*, for his interest and help. My thanks to David Morgan, who has brought contemporary psychoanalysis alive for me. A special acknowledgement is due to all the friends and family who encouraged me through my graduate study and who are an invaluable resource today, particularly my mother, and my late father, to whom this is dedicated alongside my beloved David Wootton. Thanks are also due to the family of Veronica Forrest-Thomson, and in particular to her mother, Jean, and brother, Miles. This is also for them.

The author and publishers would like to express their thanks for the following permissions:

Poems and quotations from poems by Veronica Forrest-Thomson from Veronica Forrest-Thomson, *Collected Poems and Translations*, ed. Anthony Barnett (Lewes: Allardyce, Barnett, Publishers, 1990) incorporating corrections in Veronica Forrest-Thomson, *Selected Poems*, ed. Anthony Barnett (London: Invisible Books, 1999). Copyright © Jonathan Culler and The Estate of Veronica Forrest-Thomson 1971, 1974, 1976, 1990, 1999. Printed by permission of Allardyce, Barnett, Publishers. Address enquiries c/o Allardyce, Barnett, Publishers, 14 Mount Street, Lewes, East Sussex BN7 1HL.

Quotations from Charles Bernstein, *Artifice of Absorption* (Philadelphia: Singing Horse Press/Paper Air, 1987), republished (slightly revised) in Charles Bernstein, *A Poetics* (Cambridge, MA: Harvard University Press) © by Charles Bernstein. Printed by permission of Harvard University Press.

Biographical Outline

1947   On 28 November Veronica Elizabeth Marian Forrest Thomson was born to John and Jean Forrest Thomson in Penang Maternity Hospital, Malaya, where her father was a rubber planter. Her brother Miles Thomson (her only sibling) had been born in the same hospital in 1939.

1948   The Thomson family returned from Malaya on leave and when John Forrest Thomson went back to Malaya in 1949, Miles and Veronica remained in Glasgow with their mother at her parents' home. John Forrest Thomson returned to Glasgow after the outbreak of the Malay Emergency. Veronica went to Jordanhill College School, and later to St Bride's boarding school in Helensburgh. At 16 she left school and worked for her Highers at home.

1965   Veronica left Glasgow to read English at the University of Liverpool.

1967   *Identi-kit* published under the name of Veronica Forrest, by Outposts Publications in London. On 27 April she gave a reading at the Essex Arts Festival, University of Essex, as Veronica Forrest Thomson. The announcement of her forthcoming marriage to Cavan McCarthy, poet and editor of *Tlaloc* poetry magazine, appeared in the Social and Personal column of the *Glasgow Herald*, 1 November. A cutting of this announcement (in which her name and those of her parents appeared as Forrest Thomson) in the *Tlaloc* Archive Box 3 in the Library of University College London, is annotated 'Glasgow Herald 1 NOV. '67 (All Saint's-Day!)'. Several of her early poems appeared in *Tlaloc*. She (as Veronica Forrest) and McCarthy gave a joint reading, for which a programme was produced: *Veronicavan: Program of a*

Reading at the Bristol Arts Centre, 30 December 1967.

1968 Graduated with a first class BA Honours degree from the University of Liverpool, which offered her a University Research Studentship for 1968/9, which she declined, going instead to Girton College, Cambridge. At first her PhD supervisor was the poet J. H. Prynne, who wrote a 'Personal Memoir' for inclusion in *On the Periphery*; subsequently her supervisor was Professor Graham Hough, who wrote the foreword to *Poetic Artifice*.

1970 In February *twelve academic questions* was privately published by the author – as Veronica Forrest – in Cambridge.

1971 *Language Games* (by Veronica Forrest-Thomson), published by the School of English Press at the University of Leeds, was awarded the New Poets Award 2. From this time on she consistently used the name Forrest-Thomson for her publications. Married Jonathan Culler, Fellow and Tutor of Selwyn College Cambridge (at that time also working on his PhD dissertation, and subsequently a distinguished academic and theorist), on 13 March in Cambridge, at the Registry Office on Castle Hill. Her thesis, 'Poetry as Knowledge: The Use of Science by Twentieth-Century Poets', was submitted for the PhD degree in June.

1972–4 Research Fellow in English at the University of Leicester.

1974 *Cordelia or 'A poem should not mean but be'* was published as Omens Poetry Pamphlet no. 2. Divorced from Jonathan Culler. Appointed as Lecturer in the Department of English at the University of Birmingham, and started at the University on 1 October. She bought a house in Birmingham at 55 Bull Street, Harborne.

1975 17 and 18 April, participated in Cambridge Poetry Festival, giving a reading on the first day, and taking part in the Poetry Forum on the second, with French poet Michel Couturier. She was invited to participate in, and wrote the poem 'Richard II' for *Poems for Shakespeare* (part of celebrations for Shakespeare's birthday organized by Sam Wanamaker) on 26 April: her poem was read in her absence.

Saturday, 26 April, Veronica Forrest-Thomson died in Birmingham, where the funeral was held.

1976   *On the Periphery* published by Street Editions.

1978   *Poetic Artifice: A Theory of Twentieth-Century Poetry* published by Manchester University Press.

1990   *Collected Poems and Translations*, ed. Anthony Barnett, published by Allardyce, Barnett.

Abbreviations

WORKS BY FORREST-THOMSON

C.	*Cordelia or 'A poem should not mean but be'* (Leicester: Omens, 1974)
CP	*Collected Poems and Translations*, ed. Anthony Barnett (London: Allardyce, Barnett, 1990)
IA	'Irrationality and Artifice: A Problem in Recent Poetics', *British Journal of Aesthetics*, 2 (1971), 123–33
PA	*Poetic Artifice: A Theory of Twentieth-Century Poetry* (Manchester: Manchester University Press, 1978)
PK	'Poetry as Knowledge: The Use of Science by Twentieth-Century Poets' (unpublished doctoral thesis, University of Cambridge, 1971)
SP	'The Separate Planet: John Donne and William Empson': original typescript of English version of 'La Planète séparée: John Donne et William Empson', trans. François Maguin, in *John Donne*, Cahiers de l'Herne: Les Dossiers H (Paris: l'Age d'Homme, 1983), 213–44

OTHER WORKS CITED

Barthes1	Roland Barthes, *Critical Essays*, trans. Richard Howard (Evanston, IL: Northwestern University Press, 1972)
Barthes2	Roland Barthes, *Mythologies*, trans. Annette Lavers (London: Vintage, 1993)
Barthes3	Roland Barthes, *S/Z*, trans. Richard Miller (New

	York: Hill and Wang, 1974)
Bernstein	Charles Bernstein, *Artifice of Absorption* (Philadelphia: Singing Horse Press/Paper Air, 1987), republished (slightly revised) in Charles Bernstein, *A Poetics* (Cambridge, MA: Harvard University Press, 1992), 9–89
Culler1	Jonathan Culler, *Structuralist Poetics: Structuralism, Linguistics and the Study of Literature* (London: Routledge & Kegan Paul, 1975)
Culler2	Jonathan Culler, *The Pursuit of Signs: Semiotics, Literature, Deconstruction* (London: Routledge & Kegan Paul, 1981)
Eliot1	T. S. Eliot, *Collected Poems 1909–1962* (London: Faber and Faber, 1963)
Eliot2	T. S. Eliot, 'Tradition and the Individual Talent', in *Selected Prose of T. S. Eliot*, ed. Frank Kermode (London: Faber and Faber, 1975), 37–44
Freud	Sigmund Freud, *Standard Edition of the Complete Psychological Works of Sigmund Freud*, 24 vols, trans. from the German under the general editorship of James Strachey, in collaboration with Anna Freud, assisted by Alix Strachey and Alan Tyson (London: Tavistock Publications, 1955–74)
Hejinian	Lyn Hejinian, *My Life* (Los Angeles: Sun & Moon Press, 1991)
Hutcheon	Linda Hutcheon, *A Theory of Parody: The Teachings of Twentieth-Century Art Forms* (London: Methuen, 1985)
IAT	*In the American Tree*, ed. Ron Silliman (Orono, ME: National Poetry Foundation, 1986)
Kristeva	Julia Kristeva, *Desire in Language: A Semiotic Approach to Literature and Art*, ed. Leon S. Roudiez, trans. Thomas Gora, Alice Jardine, and Leon S. Roudiez (Blackwell: Oxford, 1981)
LB	*The L=A=N=G=U=A=G=E Book*, ed. Bruce Andrews and Charles Bernstein (Carbondale: Southern Illinois University Press, 1984)
Morgan	Edwin Morgan, *Language, Poetry, and Language Poetry*, the 5th Kenneth Allott Lecture (Liverpool: Liverpool Classical Monthly, 1990)

Perelman	Bob Perelman, *The Marginalization of Poetry: Language Writing and Literary History* (Princeton, NJ: Princeton University Press, 1996)
Raitt	Suzanne Raitt, 'Veronica Forrest-Thomson *Collected Poems and Translations*', *Women: A Cultural Review*, 1:3 (1990)
Silliman	Ron Silliman, *The New Sentence* (New York: Roof Books, 1989)
Ward	Geoff Ward, *Language Poetry and the American Avant-Garde* (Keele: British Association for American Studies, 1993)
Wittgenstein1	Ludwig Wittgenstein, *Philosophical Investigations*, trans. G. E. M. Anscombe (Oxford: Blackwell, 1989)
Wittgenstein2	Ludwig Wittgenstein, *Zettel*, ed. G. E. M. Anscombe and G. H. von Wright, trans. G. E. M. Anscombe (Oxford: Blackwell, 1990)

To imagine a language means to imagine a form of life.

(Ludwig Wittgenstein, *Philosophical Investigations*)

The world is not something static, irredeemably given by a natural language. When language is re-imagined the world expands with it.

(Veronica Forrest-Thomson, *Poetic Artifice*)

For we are language   Lost
in language.

(Susan Howe, 'Speeches at the Barriers',
from *Defenestration of Prague*)

Poetry is like a swoon, with this difference:
it brings you to your senses.

(Charles Bernstein, 'The Klupzy Girl',
from *Islets/Irritations*)

Prologue

Veronica Forrest-Thomson (1947–75) was a poet, a critic, and a literary theorist who specialized in poetry and poetics. Prior to her tragically early death she had published four collections of poems, while her final collection and her major work of criticism and theory, *Poetic Artifice*, were published posthumously. In 1990 her poetry and translations, published and unpublished, were gathered together and edited into the *Collected Poems and Translations*. This invaluable edition of Forrest-Thomson's work facilitated the current resurgence in her reputation, which had been maintained throughout the intervening years by a group of poets and critics who had either known her, or been made aware of her work by those who had. The extraordinary nature of her intervention in poetry and criticism during the brief years when she was publishing has steadily been gaining recognition both in Britain and in the United States, where the writers usually known as 'Language Poets' (of whom more in chapter 5) recognized her initiatives and innovations as cousins of their own.

Poet and academic, Forrest-Thomson was writing on the cusp of the movement from modernism to postmodernism, the two most significant cultural initiatives of the century. In her critical work and her poetic technique she learnt from the former and foreshadows the latter. For the reader the experimental work of the twentieth century is inevitably challenging at first acquaintance, and correspondingly exciting as its investigations of the limitations and possibilities of language are teased out. Forrest-Thomson worked at the leading edge of poetic language and wrestled with philosophical and linguistic ideas of great complexity in the medium of poetry itself, arguably a beginning to the postmodern deconstruction of the distinctions between creative and critical writing, between the work and the theories which underpin and illuminate it.

Forrest-Thomson's aesthetic was founded on her engagement with a range of different discourses, including those of science, of philosophy, and of literary studies. In the first instance the work of British critic and poet William Empson; then Wittgenstein's philosophy of language; the work of Roland Barthes; and that of the *Tel Quel* group in Paris, were significant influences. Forrest-Thomson was well ahead of her time in discovering and employing in her poetry and critical work the theories and practices of important poststructuralist writers. The ideas and formulations of all her formative influences, which I discuss in the context of her poetry, bear on the three main themes of Forrest-Thomson's work: subjectivity, experience, and the representation of both in language. These are also important for the Language writers discussed in chapter 5.

I will trace the development of Forrest-Thomson's distinctive poetic signature, and her lasting contribution to what she – with a nice eye for an oxymoron – called 'the tradition of innovation' (*PA* 125), the characteristic twentieth-century tradition of poetry. There are fashions in literature as in other cultural productions, and poetry has, for some time, been a little out of vogue, in spite of assiduous efforts to recreate the genre, for centuries considered literature's most important and prestigious, as 'a new rock and roll'. Of course there are genuine connections – traditional as well as contemporary – between music and poetry, particularly the lyric. But the kind of writing with which I engage in this book exists to question such ready assimilations, to issue a provocation to reductive forms of classification, to interrogate speech and writing, and the very position of the speaking and writing subject through whom these are uttered.

Why is this important, over and above what Yeats called 'the fascination of what's difficult', which has a lure and an excitement all its own? Investigative writing questions and loosens the grip of cultural assumptions regarding the authenticity of speech, an unproblematic subjectivity, and the truth of experience. Through the uniquely performative – enacting what it portrays – medium of poetry, it offers us ways of exploring our most central concerns with identity and lived experience. It not only allows us to make new connections between previously disparate thoughts and feelings, but creates the possibility for what Forrest-Thomson called 'smashing and rebuilding the forms of thought' (*CP* 263) themselves, actually transforming the way we perceive, construct and represent the world by disrupting our current expectations, including those of poetry. In this the reader has a vital position: the text on the page is inactive without the reader. My readings of the work of Forrest-Thomson and the American poets are intended to open a field and chart an exploration, rather than to define, confine, or come to a conclusion.

It is worth briefly mentioning here my occasional use of psychoanalysis to discuss elements in Forrest-Thomson's poems. One of the great debates in the pairing of literature with psychoanalysis has been over how that relationship is articulated: which term is privileged, given a higher profile. Psychoanalysis has most frequently, until relatively recently, occupied the dominant position as subject, with literature as object. As Shoshana Felman remarks: 'while literature is considered as a body of *language* – to *be interpreted* – psychoanalysis is considered as a body of *knowledge*, whose competence is called upon to interpret'.[1] I too take the view that the discourse of literature is equally as deserving of the status of subject as the discourse of psychoanalysis – itself also a body of language, as Felman points out. This involves putting psychoanalytic and poetic insights into productive dialogue. In psychoanalysis, like poetry, language is pushed to its limits, and psychoanalysis is, like literary criticism, necessarily aware of its radical insufficiency as an explanatory discourse. Interpretation is irresistible and ongoing: the resistance of closure, of concluding, is at the heart of the project of contemporary investigative writing. It continues.

3

1

Identi-kit

'The question always is,' says Forrest-Thomson, 'how do poems work?' This question, posed from the outset of *Poetic Artifice*, demonstrates that for her, though the issue is a complex one, the primary focus in reading a poem must be upon process: how meaning is constructed, rather than what the poem means. Form and function – how the poem works and what it does – then become central to interpretation, rather than peripheral, although they are not ultimately separable from content and meaning. Forrest-Thomson's theoretical and critical heritage included the poet and critic William Empson, whose work she much admired. But, for her, his poetry and poetics, formalist, elegant, and intellectually demanding, shows insufficient comprehension of the important role in the future of poetry of what she characterized as the 'non-meaningful levels of poetic language, such as phonetic and prosodic patterns and spatial organisation' (*PA* xi).

The key term here, and it is one which has been contested by Language poet Charles Bernstein, is of course 'non-meaningful', and it is worth asking, as he does, how any aspect of language can be non-meaningful. Forrest-Thomson also refers to this aspect or level of language as non-semantic, or (in debate with French poet Michel Couturier at the Cambridge Poetry Festival in 1975) less intransigently as 'semi-meaningful'. This last formulation gives a clearer indication of the way in which she wanted both to use in her own poetry and to discuss in other poems the functions of the conventional techniques of poetic language: of sound, metre, rhythm, punctuation, typography, line endings and beginnings, and so on. They might then rather be described as prosthetic, or contributory to meaning, than as intrinsically meaningful.

It is with regard to the question of meaning that Forrest-Thomson also takes issue with Empson's literary criticism. Part of the problem with Empson's work is its emphasis on his innovative concept, poetic 'ambiguity'. Ambiguity, while it foreshadows the postmodern concern with polysemy, multiple meaning, is often discovered by Empson because of his primary concern with the poem's meaning, and his conviction that the meaning of a poem can be discovered by reference to the world outside the poem, while Forrest-Thomson insists that it is within the world of words, within the poem, that the poem can and must be discovered. In *Poetic Artifice* she elaborates – and it is elaborate – a system of analysis for poetry, and invents in the process a range of concepts and terms through which this analysis can be conducted. Hers is a bold, quirky, and occasionally overstated attempt to deal with an important and extremely complicated subject, but as she says in the preface:

> nothing is to be gained in this enterprise by modest disclaimers, expressions of doubts which would weigh down each paragraph. The tentative character of my proposals will be sufficiently obvious to any reader who reflects upon them and discovers their limitations and inadequacies. I am trying to devise ways of analysing the various verbal and logical devices and the literary conventions which make up poetic artifice, and if we recognise from the outset the difficulty of formulating a theory about the relations between the different strata of poetic artifice, then perhaps we may simply plunge ahead on the assumption that any theory is better than none because the disagreements it provokes will pave the way for a more adequate theory. (*PA* ix)

The prescience and practical good sense of this is borne out by Bernstein's response. I take her initiative in *Poetic Artifice* – and to some extent her recommended method of proceeding – for my own. While by no means uncritically accepting the views that poets have of their own and others' techniques and performances, my focus is on the work itself, on the poetry, on the poetics, and on their intellectual context, rather than on attempting to read life through the poems, or the poems through the life. The irresistible urge to make poetry (and other literary genres) mirror life Forrest-Thomson calls 'naturalisation', and defines as 'an attempt to reduce the strangeness of poetic language and poetic organisation by making it intelligible, by

5

translating it into a statement about the non-verbal external world' (*PA* xi). Naturalization is not only irresistible, it is clearly necessary to any critical account of poetry, which inevitably attempts to help us 'understand both poetry as an institution and individual poems as significant utterances' (*PA* xi). What Forrest-Thomson wants to suggest is that naturalization be suspended, rather than be an immediate recourse. Suspended naturalization allows the constraints imposed by the formal patterning of the poem to govern the range of interpretation, resisting the tendency to a premature narrative assimilation of the poem, particularly where that involves material imported from outside the text. What she calls 'good' or 'suspended' naturalization simultaneously relies on the connective powers of the reader and on her or his patience in their exercise. 'Learning to read poetry', she says, 'is a matter of acquiring the ability to hold together, simultaneously, continuity and discontinuity in the requisite proportions' (*PA* 21). Forrest-Thomson herself uses the restrictions placed on poetry by the conventions of language to create special effects, to challenge 'the strait-jacket of meaning' as Suzanne Raitt remarks (Raitt, 305), employing those conventions to prevent or at least impede readers in their premature rush to join words to world.

The concept of suspended naturalization – the resistance to the urge to 'reduce the strangeness' – undoubtedly owes its origins to Keats's concept of negative capability, 'when man is capable of being in uncertainties, Mysteries, doubts, without any irritable reaching after fact & reason'.[1] There is a more intimate relationship between the work of the Romantic poets – theory and practice – and that of radically innovative contemporary poetry than would at first appear, or than many practitioners would accept. This includes the persistence of the Romantic aesthetic of originality, an aesthetic which has always had a distinctly masculine bias. In a letter to me of 22 January 1995 Lyn Hejinian (herself one of the most well-known of the Language writers) recognizes this persistence of Romanticism in the course of a brief discussion of her acquaintance with Forrest-Thomson's work:

> it seems to me that a great deal of contemporary *American* poetry (the postmodern, rather than traditional poetry) is much more closely linked to English Romantic literature than is usually

acknowledged, and I suspect that this is also the case (it seems to be, but I don't want to exaggerate my familiarity with *British* poetry) there too. In Forrest-Thomson's poetry the link seems very important, not in and of itself but as a point of origin, from which a splendid and dense body of work could radiate.

Poetry as an institution is founded on its difference from prose. The nature of the difference between poetic and other forms of language, always so difficult to define, is increasingly so since the bottom line of lineation no longer offers even a barely adequate account – as the work of the Language writers attests. It is however always in part the theme of any poem, since poetry is the most self-reflexive, most self-referential of the verbal arts. This difference, marked by conventions and devices, Forrest-Thomson sums up in a word, 'artifice', frequently capitalized for emphasis in her writings; a technique familiar from poetry. If, when a poem is read, attention is paid to the different levels and devices of artifice, then readers will not be tempted to invest in ambiguities which are not relevant to and lie outside the scope of the particular utterance with which they are engaging. Nor will they prematurely seek in the world outside the text of the poem for an explanation or interpretation of what is within it.

For Forrest-Thomson a poem is primarily a fictional construct – as indeed are the other constituents of its field of operations, 'the reader' and 'the poet' – rather than an attempt to make a statement about an external situation. In *Poetic Artifice* Forrest-Thomson criticizes Empson's biographical interpretation of Donne's 'A Valediction: Forbidding Mourning' on just these grounds, remarking that 'It looks as though Donne was more concerned with writing his poem than with "soothing his wife"' (*PA* 91).[2] Her own experiments in the medium of language, except for her early and brief interest in concrete poetry – rejected precisely for its disregard of mediation – concentrate on how language itself constructs the world, rather than describes it. Concrete poets, she says, 'treat words as physical objects; they try to avoid mediation altogether' (*PA* 45); language does have a materiality, but it is neither 'the thing' itself, nor a means to get at 'things' somehow behind it. Contrary to Pound's Imagist requirement for 'direct treatment of the "thing" whether subjective or objective', this is impossible.[3]

7

As Raitt observes (Raitt, 306), the tension between subjectivity and objectivity (an inheritance from Romantic poetry's expression of the desire for fusion with the object) appears in 'Contours – Homage to Cezanne', from the first collection, *Identi-kit*:

> Objects, having nothing to express
>
> except themselves, attain intensity
> in assumed balances, which alleges,
> in face of our amorphous liberty,
> the joy of everything with edges.

(*CP* 219)

An ambivalent desire for definition, for the orderly construction of edges and lines, and paradoxically also for a Romantic dissolution of the subject, amorphous liberty and all, is a preoccupation throughout Forrest-Thomson's early poems, beginning with 'Sagittarius' (*CP* 227). One of the earliest poems we have, and certainly the earliest which shows the astonishing accomplishment of which her work was capable, it was apparently written on her nineteenth birthday under the astrological sign of Sagittarius: the manuscript bears the date '28/11/66' (*CP* 281). This sophisticated poem, which remained unpublished until the appearance of the *Collected Poems*, as we shall see introduces themes that are of importance throughout her work: the problematics of identity and experience, and the role of language in their construction.

For Forrest-Thomson, as Raitt observes, 'theories of poetry are also beliefs about identity' (Raitt, 307), a view supported by Forrest-Thomson's discussion of the relationship between poetry and identity in an explanatory note following the poetry text of the collection *Language-Games*:

> The construction of poems becomes the record of a series of individual thresholds of the experience of being conscious; they form the definition, or affirmation, in time and in language, of human identity. (*CP* 263)

Her use of the word 'thresholds' here evokes that periphery of conscious awareness, implicitly also the periphery of the unconscious, to which the title of her last collection, *On the Periphery*, also alludes. Forrest-Thomson connects the process of writing poetry with an attempt to reconstruct an experience of

8

consciousness and identity through the mediating power of language. Language is both the connection between them and the means by which the structures of consciousness, identity – and poems – are constituted.

The central question of poetics is how language mediates meaning, and 'Sagittarius' states the problem, which for poetry more acutely than for any other operation in language is one of articulation. And in addressing the subject of articulation, like Forrest-Thomson I am playing with an ambiguity of meaning in the word itself, with its dual senses of jointing or connecting different elements, and of the capacity for utterance or coherent speech.

SAGITTARIUS

Something dislocates.
I find me trying, to be
without a predicate.
For once a blueprint is no guarantee
against anonymity.

The self-set questionnaire
of circumstance
can't make all square.
Aspects jar.
A day with jagged edges and
minutes sharp to breathe through
bars retreat to neat
articulation;

derides the jingling skeletons
of sounds I blame
for these complexities:
Mercury, Moon, Jupiter,
when I was born,
were placed all wrong.
Sometimes the stars' perplexities
are fun, but now, not even names,
just pain; thoughts hurt.

The mind's an aggravated boil,
needs lancing; but no tool
– unless maybe
these jigsaw shards
of useless personality.

9

> At last I can forget
> the self-made self and work
> to turn the spheres and all
> that matters of 'I am'
> into this it
> that is.

'Something dislocates.' The poem begins with a dislocation, and something that dislocates was, by inference, once articulate or joined, jointed: mobile. Now it is out of place, out of the place where it is at home, where it belongs, and moved to another place: perhaps to what Freud designates in *The Interpretation of Dreams* as an *andere Schauplatz*, an 'other scene' (literally showplace) of the action of dreams, of the operations of the unconscious (Freud, IV, 48). And, drawing on the other sense of articulate, something is dislocated from the field of speech, is no longer speakable. The sentence order in the first stanza suggests that it is the missing predicate of line three that has dislocated, moved out of place: the predicate without which 'I find myself trying'. Here, frustrating the urge to carry on to the end of the line, the syntax allows and the punctuation insists on both interpretations for 'trying': both irritating and attempting. The absence of the predicate – the descriptive, that which is affirmed or denied of the subject by means of the copula (the verb *be* as sign of predication) – that which gives an identification or identity, makes being difficult. The position of the subject, 'I', is problematic, trying to exist without being able to say anything distinctive about that 'I' which would rescue it from anonymity, distinguish it. The subject finds itself as an object ('I find me'), and particularly its lack of identity, difficult to bear.

The characteristic tremendous compression of sense here and the same issue of verbal connection also appear in a subsequent poem, 'Antiquities', concerned with very similar linguistic and psychic issues:

> Glance is the copula
> that petrifies our several identities,
> syntactic superficies.

(*CP* 31)

'Antiquities' is a poem in which metaphoric relations are rendered concrete by the use of the copula, by the logical

10

process of predication: it begins 'A gesture is adjective...' and continues 'A mirror is a museum-case...' 'Emotion is a parenthesis'. The manipulation of syntax, to which added attention is drawn by using the word 'syntactic', doubles the sense of the lines as in 'Saggitarius'. The glance petrifies: the gaze both fixes and terrifies its object; and the suggestion is that it terrifies precisely because it fixes. Forrest-Thomson constructs a brief but brilliant argument in poetic language, demonstrating the performativity of which it is capable, and a chilling, glittering metaphorical insight into the paradoxical provisionality of what we call 'identity'.

According to Lacan, the child's first perception of identity at the Mirror Stage – a development of Freud's earlier theory of narcissism: 'love directed towards the image of oneself'[4] – essentially devolves upon the gaze of the self as viewed, frozen as it were, in a mirror, or perhaps as reflected in the gaze of the mother. It involves a specular identification of subject and object that does not discriminate between the two linguistically significant positions, and which is founded on a fundamental error: the misrecognition of the self as more unified than it actually can be before the infant develops motor coordination. And we cannot forget the psychoanalytic association of the gaze with castration: looking and seeing can present the most terrifying of gendered threats based on a phantasy of the meaning of sexual difference, and yet they are also vitally constitutive of the subject.

Forrest-Thomson's metaphysical conceit (and Donne, like Empson is an important precursor) creates a Gorgon whose power can frighten and freeze – petrify – whose gaze can be the 'copula' that connects as it turns to stone our 'several', that is both multiple and separate (another doubling), 'identities'. Identities which are, like part of the poetic art which informs Forrest-Thomson's lines, 'syntactic superficies', or clever arrangements of surfaces. Through the manipulation of the formal elements of language, utterance is given to that which cannot be spoken directly, for the want of a form of articulation that can capture the duplicities or multiplicities of identity; the paradoxes of being.

The abrupt and awkward punctuation of the first stanza of 'Sagittarius' enacts just this sense of hiatus, blockage, and

11

disruption, by means of which 'retreat to neat/articulation', to facile transcriptions of meaning, is barred. The 'jingling' – articulated – 'skeletons/of sounds' may be blamed, but not outmanoeuvred, for language is itself constitutive of identity. Throughout her work Forrest-Thomson makes striking use of the phonic level of language as part of her arsenal of artifice – 'Mercury, Moon, Jupiter' – and is always acutely sensitive to the use of sound by other poets. This is in part an inheritance from the Russian Formalists, through the work of Roman Jakobson, and is one of the important features that connects her work with Bernstein's, and with that of Barrett Watten, for whom the Formalists are an important theoretical source.

'Anonymity' suggests that namelessness hints at non-existence, and at the least the lack of an individual identity. It suggests too the fear of failing to establish originality through the painful continuous process of constructing 'the self-made self': we cannot forget that the forgotten individual poet has her or his poems signed 'Anon'. Even a blueprint – and the technical language is itself distancing – offers only a plan, no elevation: it is two-dimensional, just the outline; a stereotypical image like that produced by the identikit process; like the astrological chart from which Forrest-Thomson quotes. The attempt to 'make all square', to square the circle of circumstance – or here the circular form of a natal astrological chart, appropriately enough for a birthday poem – is bound to fail: defining the individual as the sum of her or his experiences is inadequate. Sometimes astrology is fun, but not on a 'day with jagged edges', so sharp one can cut oneself. Sharp like each minute, in both senses of one sixtieth of an hour and of a fraction of an angular degree, and there are 21,600 of these slivers in a circle, in an astrological chart. They are as painful to endure as the sharpness of breathing, like knives in the chest, after running, or when afraid. 'Aspects jar' invokes the astrological theory that a system of correspondences – positive or negative – between planets in different positions is thought to presage the character of the subject of the horoscope: another technology which is inadequate to the task of defining the subject. These scraps of lines – blueprint, astrological chart, poem, like the identikit which entitles her first collection – offer no defence 'against anonymity'; no passport to identity and significance, let alone immortality: the desire for which, the immortality of the text, is such a traditional and powerful theme of poetry. Desire also encompasses death, desire's end, of which oblivion or forgetting is the precursor:

> At last I can forget
> the self-made self and work
> to turn the spheres and all
> that matters of 'I am'
> into this it
> that is.

The 'self-made self' gets no further description than the deep relief of forgetting, relinquishing it, turning to the narrowing compass of the last three lines where the emphasis falls successively on ' "I am" ', 'it' and 'is'. This images the dissolution of 'the self-made self', that can say by virtue of the effort that went into making it 'I am' (first person singular), into the neutrality and impersonality of the third person: 'it is'. Turning everything of being, of subjectivity, back into the simplest of possible objective descriptions: 'it is'.

In 'In the Greenhouse', from *Identi-kit*, the perilous painful pleasures of the dissolution of self that are courted in 'Sagittarius' are invoked as a kind of vegetable love, blurring definitions, banishing the capacity for thought which makes the distinction between 'plant and primate'. Forrest-Thomson alliteratively images this as a consummation devoutly to be wished in the final stanza of a poem which Edwin Morgan in his review at the time rightly called 'a sort of Marvellian meditation':[5]

> The silent rhythm of pulsating pores
> filling my lungs with filtered earth
> is all I feel or know of alien shapes
> that once were flowers.
> I breathe their breath
> until all definitions are dissolved,
> and homo sapiens is nothing more to me.

> (CP 209)

Forrest-Thomson metaphysically invokes the discourse of science (her doctoral thesis was on the use of science in twentieth-century poetry) within that of poetry in a manner strongly reminiscent of Empson's poetry. She plays on the oxygen/carbon dioxide cycle of exchange between plant and human respiration systems, but a shade of ambiguity hovers over this particular 'exchange'. This 'I' breathes the breath of the vegetation and dissolves its humanity: thanatos imagined as resolving the struggle of human consciousness and individuation. Only if 'homo sapiens' inhales carbon dioxide like plants, rather than the oxygen exhaled by plants, will dissolution or death result. These lines hold an echo of Marvell's 'The Garden', where the mind is imaged as: 'Annihilating all that's made / To a green Thought in a green Shade'.[6] Forrest-Thomson is slowly and subtly developing through her early poems the technique of allusion which will later evolve into a complex and sophisticated parodic technique.

Until the publication of *Language-Games*, her poems appeared under the name 'Veronica Forrest'. Forrest-Thomson's idiosyncratic use of the hyphen in her name came later, but an interest in the device is clear from the title of her first collection. *Identi-kit* is a play on the name of the police method of developing a composite picture of a wanted person: a wanted person who could here be either self or other. This forms part of the search for a poetic 'subject' – in both senses – which subtends the field of her poetry. The quest for the other explicitly underlies her final, posthumous collection, *On the Periphery*, as its preface reveals:

> this book is the chart of three quests. The quest for a style already discussed, the quest for a subject other than the difficulty of writing, and the quest for another human being. (CP 264)

'Identi-kit' is conspicuously hyphenated, against custom, and this inscription of difference within similarity increases the typographical impact of the hyphen itself, simultaneously drawing attention to the split she has created and attempting to bridge it. Forrest-Thomson investigates this in her later poem on the subject, 'The Hyphen':

> i hyphen (Gk. together, in one)
> a short dash or line used to connect
> two words together as a compound [...]
> But also: to divide
> for etymological or other purpose.

(CP 35)

Typically, as in 'Sagittarius', the line breaks are used to

underline the theme: 'connect/ two words', and 'divide/ for etymological or other purpose'. As to purpose, in the case of 'Identi-kit' this is an effective device to focus attention on the elements of the word, at once discrete and united. It serves, introducing her first published collection, to emphasize the theme of identity, and also to indicate the possibility of discovering or creating a kit of tools for its investigation. Language, particularly poetic language, that is language shaped by poetic artifice, is to be the toolkit with which to construct and explore both identity and experience: 'The basis of continuity between poetry and the rest of one's experience is the essentially verbal nature of that experience: the fact that it takes shape through language. What we can know of experience always lies within language.' (*PA* 20)

Her title-poem has the familiar structure of the Shakespearean sonnet, though with some variation:

IDENTI-KIT

Love is the oldest camera.
Snap me with your eyes.
Wearied with myself I want
a picture that simplifies.

Likeness is not important
provided the traits cohere.
Dissolve doubts and contradictions
to leave the exposure clear.

Erase shadows and negative
that confuse the tired sight.
Develop as conclusive definition
a pattern of black and white.

For I wish to see me reassembled
in that dark-room of your mind.

(*CP* 208)

It is immediately clear that Forrest-Thomson is addressing the issue of representation. An identikit picture is not a portrait, not even a sketch: it is a stereotypical image created in the absence of the subject, an improvization based on the slender evidence of memory. It invites a partial rather than full recognition, drawing attention to both the provisionality of identity and its construction in the mind of the other. The intended end of the identikit process, constructed in the absence of a clearly identifiable subject, is the resolution of identification in the photograph taken of the arrested person, after the discovery of the 'true' identity of the subject, tentatively recorded in their absence. The narrative withheld from the observer in the composite picture built up of lines is filled out in the photographic representation. Forrest-Thomson's interest in this development from the graphic to the photographic image, this metaphorical progression, is recorded here and further developed in the later 'Ducks & Rabbits' where the photograph remains withheld, implied rather than overt. The importance of metaphors of visual imagery in these early poems demonstrates Forrest-Thomson's concern with perception.

She extracts fresh life from the old trope of love's blindness by eliding the gaze of love with the camera: 'Love is the oldest camera./Snap me with your eyes.' Love is the oldest camera, recorder of the beloved's image; bringing to mind the 'camera obscura' (literally 'dark room') from which the photographic camera gets its name: a 'darkened box with aperture for projecting image of distant object on screen'. Again we have the tension, the distance between subject and object, linked with the idea of projection, and with the wearying process of being a subject, desiring the resolution of the complexities of identity into a simple, coherent, 'black and white' picture. With no shades of grey, this is an idealized image, as the images of love always needs must be, in the same way that the allegory of the Mirror Stage describes a move that misrepresents and idealizes the ego. Implicit in the 'I' of the poem's 'wish to see me reassembled' is a sense of self as provisional, fragmented, like the infant's experience of the *corps morcelé*, the body in pieces, prior to its premature unification in the gaze. It is thus appropriate, though sinister, that this should take place in the 'dark-room', where a photograph is developed from negative to positive image, of the mind of the other: reassembled in the image of the other's desire.

The 'still' camera, of course, employs monocular vision, and monocular vision erases depth, records everything in the same plane: it flattens out the subject to give precisely 'a picture that simplifies'. And a picture is a two-dimensional surface, like a page of text: a page of lines, of black and white, like the identikit

16

picture, or like the blueprint and astrological chart of 'Sagittarius'. Like these, the identikit picture is a system of lines, constructing an imaginary subject: the poetic persona is clearly a fictional construct. This text on the page also indicates an absence: that of a clearly identifiable speaking subject; for who is the 'I' set up by the poem? 'Identi-kit''s theme is recapitulated in the final couplet, where the desire to escape the self and its complexities that appeared in 'Sagittarius' appears again (as it will do in 'Gemini' from the same collection).

The problem is how to identify a self that can operate in a world where boundaries are shifting and conclusions temporary. The infant (*infans*: literally 'unable to speak') can only distinguish itself from the rest of the world by the symbolizing capacity that forms the foundation of language. This capacity for fantasy, another word for symbolization, seems to be innate. Fantasy constitutes the infant as the centre of the universe, a centrality which is gradually deferred and decentred as reality impinges on the imaginary, as when hallucinated satisfaction in the absence of the breast proves to be an empty experience, leading to the recognition of the existence of the separate other. In 'Sagittarius' Forrest-Thomson deploys a self-centred view of the universe: an omnipotence, however anxious, in which everything revolves about the subject, where the 'I' in the text sets up a relationship with, indeed calls into being, the other – which of course includes the reader. 'Identi-kit' engages with an-other, but only instrumentally, as an enablement towards the dissolution of self and its reconstitution as the desire of the other. In 'Gemini', also from *Identi-kit*, as we might expect from the Zodiac sign of the twins, there are textually two:

GEMINI

When all's said and spun,
heads or tails?
it's all two
for I am a pun
on someone unknown.

My life's his uncracked code.
Pleasure consists only in deflecting
the signals he transmits,
trying to flex his wit reflected
through my reflexes.

Thus we play a game
in which each day is a lost bet,
for how, when I must use his words,
can I communicate my paradox
to a distinctive third.

I'll never break true the mirror
that lies in each it and you,
in which I can see just me,
watching him,
watching me.

(*CP* 206)

There are textually two, but one is the mirror (impervious, reflexive) for the other: 'I'll never break true the mirror/that lies in each it and you'. For this subject, this 'I', each object ('it and you') is a mirror. A mirror which is 'true' gives no distortion to the image it reflects; and with the pun on 'true' and 'through' – a gesture towards Alice's passage 'Through the Looking Glass', and the mirror which shattered when the Lady of Shalott looked directly at the world rather than its reflection – Forrest-Thomson implicitly calls into question the 'truth' of this reflection and reflecting surface, inevitably again invoking the Mirror Stage. While Forrest-Thomson is unlikely to have read Lacan's account of this before writing these poems (though she certainly did read the *Écrits* by the early seventies at the latest), the essentials of his formulation – which Lacan elaborated from Kojève's lectures on Hegel – have been in circulation for rather longer. The literary tropes which play with mirrors have of course been with us for longer still.

At the Mirror Stage, prior to the actual development of motor coordination in its own body, the infant experiences an intensely pleasurable mastery of the movements of its reflection, and in this situation of the infant's love relation with the idealized image of its unified body lies an alienation fundamental to Lacan's theorization of the subject. Thus, for Lacan, narcissism rather than relation founds the subject. The split in consciousness occasioned by the original *méconnaissance*, misrecognition of the subject itself as unified, and the concomitant alienation of the subject problematizes identity. A subjectivity founded on irrecoverable loss is indeed difficult to come to terms with; an irrecoverable loss, moreover, of that which was never actually possessed in the first place.

18

What one knows, that is the means by which an experience is known to consciousness, is necessarily partial and distorted. The very existence of an unconscious means that in order to attempt to 'know thyself' one must first accept that there is an immensity of the self (and by the same token of the other) that is not only unknown but which perhaps remains ultimately unknowable. For both Freud and Lacan the only units of meaning to escape from the unconscious into consciousness are those which obtrude from the unconscious in the forms of dreams, slips of the tongue, or jokes. In 'Gemini' – a poem thematically concerned with the masochistically pleasurable constraints of language – as in 'Identi-kit', there are language play, puns and wit, and perhaps something more: the construction of the poem as a net to catch the slippery and elusive unconscious processes, the restless metonymies of desire.

From the outset Forrest-Thomson puts a linguistic spin on the triteness of the proverbial in a doubling movement of citation and subversion such as we might expect from a poem about the Twins, relishing the slipperiness of language. The punning flip from the expected 'when all's said and done' to 'when all's said and spun' (which rhymes both visually and phonically with 'pun' in line four) mimes the spinning coin's oscillating wager: 'heads or tails?' The result of which is 'all two' rather than 'all one' which would complete both sense and rhyme. The comic-ironic language play prevalent in the work of this period – which includes poems which rework wise saws and modern instances like 'Don't Bite the Hand that Throws Dust in Your Eyes', full of proverbs with a twist in the tale – demonstrates a delight in dodging the restrictions imposed by using pre-cast elements of language.

In 'Gemini', 'I am a pun/on someone unknown', rather than having an individual identity. The poem moves from this linguistically playful but painful evocation of the subject as a linguistic incursion from the unconscious (reinforced by the rhyme of 'pun' with 'someone'), through an image of desire activated in imitation of the other – as in the mirror – where:

> Pleasure consists only in deflecting
> the signals he transmits,
> trying to flex his wit reflected
> through my reflexes.

The pleasure (and the identity) is clearly one of reaction rather than action. Rather perversely this pleasure comes from deflecting rather than reflecting the signals of the unknown (except that he is masculine) other. The first line of this verse, 'My life's his uncracked code', also suggests living only through, and perhaps for, the beloved other; the relinquishing of individuation, the loss of identity and self. That loss of identity being the paradoxical pleasure of sexuality, the tantalizing promise of blissful merging. And how impossible to register in language the nature of an identity which is already at least two removes from the subject, which is an-other's 'uncracked code', an impenetrable secret language, in which 'I' must use his woefully inadequate words, having no language of my own:

> for how, when I must use his words,
> can I communicate my paradox
> to a distinctive third.

This perfect description of the paradoxical nature of the psycho-analytic situation also conveys the necessity for the subject – for any subject – to use a language not their own. It is tempting to read this as a statement about gender, that the female has no language of her own, but to assume that this voice is female is to assume coincidence of the gender of the author with that of the 'I' of the poem. This would be a less contentious move in a poem less explicitly themed. The original Twins of the Zodiac, the inseparable Dioscuri, were both male.[7] And the relationship that has been most readily open to the charge of narcissism is that between members of the same sex. A poem about twins is inevitably dealing with splitting: identical or monozygotic twins develop from a split ovum. But who is the 'distinctive third', the element separate from this binary? I suggest that this 'third' represents the third term that is inevitably produced by any form of splitting, as when an object is split into good and bad, setting up the triangle of subject and good and bad objects; a process which does not require the usual specification of gender. This complex (and basically Kleinian) negotiation of splitting and projection, articulates a process of relationship which does not require the making of a presumption of gender. Splitting and projection are of course an alternative to dissolution for the relinquishing of personal identity.

Forrest-Thomson deliberately avoids the conventional question mark, as she will for another rhetorical question on the subject of truth in a later poem, 'S/Z':

> What is true.
> I write no question mark
> after that question.
>
> (CP 112)

The rhetorical question posed in 'Gemini' also constructs its own answer, and reflects the impossibility of seeking the truth of the self in the other, the imaginary counterpart originated in the Mirror Stage. It is this imaginary counterpart through whom the desire of the subject – and thus the subject – is alienated, which is subsequently projected onto the narcissistically cathected love object:

> I'll never break true the mirror
> that lies in each it and you,
> in which I can see just me,
> watching him,
> watching me.

According to Lacan, the subject's truth and hence the subject's identity is not to be found in the ego, the place of the subject's alienated desires, but in the locus of the Other, which is that of the unconscious. This is not easily reached because of the essentially disturbing nature of truth, which only slips out in dreams, jokes, and parapraxes. And perhaps too, as I have suggested, through the experience of a poetry which is 'the record of a series of individual thresholds of the experience of being conscious' (CP 263).

The focus here has been on how, from the beginning of her adult poetic work, the theme of the search for – and construction of – identity in language was central to Forrest-Thomson's work. Next I will discuss a theme which is equally central: that of the transformation of experience into art, and in particular into the art of language, which also subtends her poetry and poetics.

21

2

Language-Games

I remember the shock of recognition I felt when Edwin Morgan and I gave her the award in the second Leeds New Poets' Competition in 1971, for her *Language Games*. These austerely garnished found-poems should have been frigid and un-approachable, but were the opposite – fantastic and frightening.

(Peter Porter)

Beginning in France with the ideas that informed structuralism, an enormous revolution in the conditions of knowledge in the human sciences took place during the 1960s and through the 1970s, matching the political and social unrest of the period which in Paris culminated in the *événements* of May 1968. Though not notably politically inclined, unlike the Language writers, nor sharing Language writing's project of social transformation, Forrest-Thomson gestures towards these events at the end of her 'Note' to the collection *Language-Games*. When discussing the necessity for 'smashing and rebuilding the forms of thought' in the medium of poetry, she remarks that 'one might be permitted to feel a certain affinity with those who see the role of the University as a subversion of accepted social reality' (*CP* 263). The idea that what were previously known as 'fields of knowledge', such as science, philosophy, medicine, and aesthetics, are constructed by the systems of language which purport to analyse them, became increasingly a focus of interest in the attempt to interrogate and subvert not just 'accepted social reality' but the notion of 'reality' itself. These discourses, which in their simpler forms Wittgenstein would have called different language-games, create apparently objec-tive self-ratifying descriptions of reality, descriptions which both define the object of their enquiry (their subject), and construct the modes of thought by which a conceptual analysis of that object may be made. Forrest-Thomson was becoming increasingly interested in the possibilities of such language-systems for poetry, and by 1971, at a time when most British and American theorists were just beginning to get to grips with structuralism, while in France its moment was passing, she was already declaring herself to be a poststructuralist, thus placing herself in the vanguard of what has come to be known as 'theory'.[1] In her writings of this period we can see the gradual inauguration of new ways of thinking about, analysing, and writing poetry and poetics, informed by poststructuralist insights into discursive practices, the condition of the subject, and her or his possibilities of experience.

But when Forrest-Thomson went up to Cambridge in 1968 to begin her PhD at Girton College, where initially the poet Jeremy Prynne was her supervisor (later replaced by Graham Hough), the philosophy of Wittgenstein permeated the intellectual life of the university, as the poet Denise Riley recalls in a letter to me of 17 May 1994: 'Certainly tons of Wittgenstein got read. V's style in these earliest poems is very like Wittgenstein's voice in his half-tentative, half-assured self-notations in The Blue and Brown Books and elsewhere: Wittgenstein's is a catchy tone and Veronica perhaps caught it then.' The colloquial tone of some of the poems in *Identi-kit* already has some of the vernacular catchiness that Forrest-Thomson clearly found so congenial in Wittgenstein. The 'voice' that Riley registers stems from his use of everyday speech in preference to specialized philosophical discourse, since the purpose of philosophy, according to Wittgenstein, is to 'battle against the bewitchment of our intelligence by means of language' (Wittgenstein1, 47:109).[2] However, particularly in the works that follow the *Tractatus Logico-Philosophicus*, the apparent simplicity of Wittgenstein's formulations is deceptive. As when reading Forrest-Thomson's poetry, it is far easier to understand the sense of the words than to be sure that one has grasped his meaning, and, as David Pears notes, 'in his later philosophy it is always easier to understand what he is saying than it is to understand the point of his saying it'.[3] The apparent transparency of Wittgenstein's language is belied by the complexity of the conceptual structure it is intended to convey, and in this subtle form of division by a shared language lies a paradox in itself attractive to a poet so

23

concerned with the capacities and limitations of language.

The poems in *Language-Games*, which appeared in 1971, were written between 1968 and 1969. The first thirteen poems in the collection had already been self-published – with the addition of 'Variations from Sappho' as initial poem, subsequently excluded from *Language-Games* – as *twelve academic questions* (1970). This typically playfully perverse title of course begs a question itself, one worth keeping in mind when reading these poems: given that there were fourteen poems, what were the questions? And why was 'Sappho' excluded from the later grouping, as 'Sagittarius' was excluded from *Identi-kit*, while its formal sophistication, imagery, and typography easily merit publication (it is arguably superior to many of the poems included in *Identi-kit*)? In 'Sagittarius', the 'I' set up by the poem may have seemed too personal, and the affective (emotional) rawness too close to the work of the so-called 'confessional' poets whose 'introversion' she deplored in 'An Impersonal Statement' (*CP* 260). This – written in the third person to construct the impersonality its title invokes – appeared in *Veronicavan*, published in 1967 (the same year as *Identi-kit*) as part of a programme for a performance of work by herself and Cavan McCarthy, editor of *Tlaloc*, to whom she had been formally engaged.

Perhaps, also, the poem may have seemed too close to biography, too self-absorbed to one who at this stage – and theoretically at least – so relished the artistic 'impersonality' that T. S. Eliot had prescribed in his 'Tradition and the Individual Talent', an essay that had a pronounced influence on Forrest-Thomson's thinking, as indeed it had on that of many poets and critics. However in *Veronicavan* she herself attributes her 'perhaps exaggerated, respect for impersonality and formal values in art' at this point, which caused her to react not only against the confessional poets but also against 'the formlessness and academicism of the Movement writers', to 'an early specialisation in Greek and Latin' rather than to Eliot (*CP* 260). 'Sappho' may have been excluded for similar reasons, although it is always possible that the author simply felt that it was less appropriate to the theme of *Language-Games* than the other poems from *twelve academic questions*, a group of poems whose complexities raise rather more than a dozen queries.

Anthony Barnett, editor of the *Complete Poems and Translations*, certainly thinks that Forrest-Thomson's mature *oeuvre* begins with *Language-Games*, as he explains in a prefatory 'Editor's Note'. Barnett suggests that 'had she lived, the author might not have wished to reprint the majority of her poems from that earlier period', and in his edition they are placed 'following the poems written or published in the 1970s' (*CP* 12). 'Variations from Sappho' is actually the last poem of his edition. I understand Barnett's caution, both as an editor and as a poet himself, but in terms of their formal experimentation and their thematic content – intendedly not always clearly differentiated features – and despite the *longueurs* of some experiments with concrete or sound poetry such as 'Atomic Disintegration' (*CP*240-1), these poems more than merit consideration as foundational to Forrest-Thomson's poetics and later poetry: a number are valuable in their own right.

'Variations from Sappho' is deliberately fragmented, on the model of the fragmentary remains of Sappho's own writings. Some of Sappho's poems were found on papyri used to wrap mummies, and as Willis Barnstone remarks:

> many were torn in vertical strips, and as a result the Sappho fragments are mutilated at the beginning or end of lines, if not in the middle. The mummy-makers of Egypt transformed much of Sappho into columns of words, syllables, or single letters, and so made her poems look, at least typographically, like Apollinaire's or e.e.cummings' shaped poems... But the price of this unwitting modernization was the loss of intelligibility of many fragments.[4]

These fragments, with their enforced 'modernization' of the earliest celebrated woman poet, have been pieced together by scholars in attempts to 'read' the poems as more complete utterances, often by filling in some of the missing bits. This sounds remarkably like Freud's account of the work of psycho-analysis, the talking cure, and its rearticulations of the fragmentary recollections or associations of patients:

> psychogenic material is... drawn through a narrow cleft and thus arrives in consciousness cut up, as it were, into pieces or strips. It is the psychotherapist's business to put these together once more into the organization which he presumes to have existed. (Freud, II, 291)

The process is also reminiscent of the practice of the literary critic, notably with the kind of modern and modernist works to which Barnstone refers, and of later texts, like those of Forrest-Thomson and the Language writers, which employ fragmentation and discontinuity as part of their technical vocabulary.

Part of Forrest-Thomson's 'Sappho' poem is a direct quotation from Sappho's poem 'To Eros', a one-line fragment: 'You burn me',[5] on which she plays variations similar to those seen in the Russian Futurist *zaum* poetry, by shifting one phonemic element of a word at a time:

> You burn me
> Yu born my
> o   u   y
> You bore me
> w   h   y

(*CP* 258)

As Peter Nicholls observes, ' "Transrational language [*zaum*]" is based on the principle that letters have a meaning independent of the words in which they appear. They can therefore be recombined to produce words which, while they belong to no known language, still mean something'.[6] While Forrest-Thomson plays with such ideas in both poetry and poetics (as when discussing 'our favourite key of *o*' in *Poetic Artifice* (*PA* 108)), here the engagement with meaning is not only at the level of the phoneme but also at the level of the signifier. The 'Oh you why?' of the vowel play in the third line leads into a telling doubling of meaning in which 'bore' in the sense of weary slides into 'bore' in the sense of engender. For the earlier poet can be seen as the forebear of the modern one, as each poet gives birth to the poetic subject. Some of Sappho's loveliest lines are written about a small daughter, and this fragment from Forrest-Thomson ends in that most poignant of questions, especially for a mother from a child: why was I born?

Barnstone writes, romantically enough, that 'in Sappho we hear for the first time in the Western world the direct words of an individual woman. It is the lyric voice in solitude.'[7] His unproblematic assimilation of the poet Sappho to the 'I' of her poems is a move that Forrest-Thomson would not make, and one of which all readers need to be wary, but the affective content released from a poem in a reading is not something from which we should recoil. As she says in *Poetic Artifice*, 'it is not entirely clear why we should want to do away with the notion that there is feeling in poetry, for we should find ourselves very quickly arguing that poetry is of no interest at all' (*PA* 18–19). But the emotion with which Forrest-Thomson is concerned, and which remains the genuine province of interest of the readers of poetry, is the emotion that comes from the interaction of the words and the poetic artifice within the poem: what Forrest-Thomson a little stiffly calls 'the interactions between the various levels of language that make up a technique' (*PA* 38). This is unlocked by a reading which resists external naturalization, which stays within the poem, and which subscribes to a – poststructuralist – relational rather than referential theory of meaning. One in which words have their meaning by juxtaposition with other words, rather than by reference to external objects. This avoids, as so-called 'bad' or premature naturalization does not, the production of an affective 'message' which would personalize the poem as an emotional release or recollection by the poet, rather than finding the affect the product of the poem itself as a linguistic construct. Forrest-Thomson's position is clear: any emotional or other relationship to experience is mediated by the poem.

Forrest-Thomson's use of brackets in the final section, which also tells a fragmentary and reconstructed story, imitates that of the classical scholars in their attempted recuperations of Sappho's work:

> a(ll) mi(xed)
> te(ll) tongue (me)
> tell to(ngue) ( )
> t(all)
> les(s)

To reconstruct anew: 'All mixed in the telling of the tongue (a synecdoche for speech) are "tall tales"'. All poets tell such tall tales (contemporary poets in particular tell fragmentary narratives), and all identity in poetry is fictional, however 'historical' or even autobiographical the poem may seem. 'Variations from Sappho' is a reminder of this, a memorialization of the work of probably the most fictionalized of all women poets, of whose identity so little is known, much of whose work is preserved in tantalizing fragments.

Forrest-Thomson's aesthetic and the poetry of this period are clearly founded on her engagement with Wittgenstein's work on language, as the title of her collection *Language-Games* declares. In this collection, the first published under her chosen hyphenated name, the title follows the pattern of Wittgenstein's own idiosyncratic use of the hyphen in the *Philosophical Investigations* to create a compound expression from the two words; in the earlier *Blue and Brown Books* they were discrete. This creates additional significance for the term, making it more distinctive than an aggregate of the two separate lexical units. The special relevance of Wittgenstein's language-game theory to Forrest-Thomson's work lies in the fact that the language-game not only involves the words, but the total behavioural context in which they are used – what Forrest-Thomson refers to in 'The Hyphen' as 'the "context in which we occur"/that teaches us our meaning'. 'I shall...call the whole', says Wittgenstein, 'consisting of language and the actions into which it is woven, the "language-game"'. (Wittgenstein1, 5:7)

For Wittgenstein, 'like everything metaphysical the harmony between thought and reality is to be found in the grammar of the language' (Wittgenstein2, 11:55): the relationship between inner and outer worlds (or text and context) is to be discovered in the logical relations or system of language. Wittgenstein uses the game of chess as a metaphor to illustrate his discussion of the rules of language, rules which he regards – as Saussure regards the connection between sign and referent – as arbitrary: 'if you follow other rules than those of chess you are *playing another game*; and if you follow grammatical rules other than such-and-such ones, that does not mean you say something wrong, no, you are speaking of something else' (Wittgenstein2, 58:320). His investigations led him to suggest that when problems of communication and understanding arise, rather than being founded on the breaking of the rules of discourse, they are an effect of words being used in different language-games.

This insight he appropriately enough formulated for poetry as: 'Do not forget that a poem, even though it is composed in the language of information, is not used in the language-game of giving information' (Wittgenstein2, 27:160). Forrest-Thomson plays with this when she takes dictionary definitions – clearly written in the language-game of giving information – and turns them into poetry, as she does in 'The Hyphen', and in 'Michaelmas', the first poem of *Language-Games*. Her appropriation of material from other discourses, including that of philosophy, is part of a project to renew and extend the possibilities of the discourse of poetry, and she describes her programme for this in a 'Note' following the poems in *Language-Games*:

> There is the opportunity to turn theoretical debate and abstract statement into a means of technical experiment in the actual medium of poetry, to explore new formal possibilities while extending the range of material dealt with. This involves an assimilation, not merely of the ideas but of the speech-forms of the relevant areas of discourse and even their methods of typographical layout. Certain poems here tentatively explore such possibilities. It will be seen that this leads to a new stress on the importance of 'subject' in a poem; but because it is not the ideas merely but the actual linguistic forms that are to be the object of attention, the new kind of subject will be one that can be approached and even defined in terms of formal experimentation. (*CP* 262–3)

How might this work in practice? The subject of 'The Hyphen' is at first sight obvious, developed as it is from an *OED* definition (*CP* 35). But the poem (dedicated 'For the centenary of Girton College') is also about the college building itself, part of which, called the Hyphen, was built in the 1930s 'to connect Chapel Wing and Library' as she says.[8] To address this double subject the poem figures a range of gaps and their closures, physical and metaphorical, and ends with a 'state-/ ment of our need to hyphenate.' That is to yoke things – and people – subjects and objects together, however provisionally. Here the line break between these final lines, exposing the hyphen, is determined by a formal imperative. There needs must be a hyphen at the close of this centenary poem, to mirror what Forrest-Thomson calls the 'lacunae/ of a century', imaged at the beginning of the poem by the brief lines '1869-/ 1969', lines which feature the hyphen as connector and divider of the years, spanning those lacunae. Forrest-Thomson's characteristic use of the allegedly 'non-meaningful' aspects of language, on this occasion principally typography and layout, materially and figuratively constructs the meaning, or rather what she called the thematic synthesis or 'the design of the whole' (*PA* 131). This synthesis, which is ultimately produced by a careful reading of all the linguistic elements and forms in a poem, far exceeds the simple subject suggested by the title, 'The Hyphen'. By such manoeuvres form and content become indivisible and equal in importance in the text of the poem. This is 'another aspect of that rule of Artifice, of "content as form": that form becomes content' (*PA* 148).

During this period at Cambridge Forrest-Thomson also completed her PhD thesis, 'Poetry as Knowledge: The Use of Science by Twentieth-Century Poets', which was submitted in the June of 1971, the year of publication of *Language-Games*. Wittgenstein's theory of the language-game also explains the connection between her theoretical work and her contemporary poetry. In both cases at least one other language-game is united with that of poetry: in the former science, and in the latter philosophy. Her thesis investigates the way material from the discourse of science is taken up and reinflected in the field of poetry by, in particular, Pound, William Carlos Williams, and Empson. Although their use of material from another language-game was chiefly for the metaphorical potential of science as an epistemology, and as a discursive practice, it is also clear that the importation of such a discourse can illuminate the formal practices of poetry which can be naturalized within the canonical discourse of the poetry, and hence lost to sight and consciousness. That is, it can illuminate the enduring questions: what makes poetry different from other forms of language-use? and, how do poems work?

Her choice of research project already demonstrates Forrest-Thomson's concern with the power of discourse to construct, not simply analyse, a field of knowledge. And with the central implication of another poststructuralist concept, intertextuality, that no text stands in isolation. This is particularly clear in texts which use devices such as allusion, translation, quotation, parody and pastiche, whether consciously or unconsciously employed, like many of her own poems; but the multiple relationships and structures of relationship within and between texts also involve transpositions of signifying systems from one discourse to another. A major concomitant of this way of thinking about texts is that they are primarily seen as self-reflexive (writing about writing), or in reference to other texts, rather than to some external reality. Intertextuality, an increasingly important concept for her work, clearly relates to Forrest-Thomson's interest in the language-game, to her concern with premature naturalization by reference to a world outside the words of the poem, and also to what she calls the 'underlying theme' of the poems in *Language-Games*: 'the impossibility of expressing some non-linguistic reality, or even of experiencing such a reality' (CP 261–2). Clearly she developed this insight from Wittgenstein's famous statement in the *Tractatus* that '*The limits of my language* mean the limits of my world' (his italics),[9] to which she alludes in her contributor's note to *Solstice* (CP 261), and the Note to *Language-Games* (CP 261–2) which was developed from it, and which she subsequently quotes in *Poetic Artifice* (PA 20).

Citations of this statement, important for her work and for that of successive avant-garde poets and theorists,[10] usually elide both the fact that here Wittgenstein is specifically discussing *factual* language, which explicitly excludes ethics, metaphysics, and, most significantly, aesthetics, and that the statement belongs to a period in Wittgenstein's philosophy when he assumed that, as David Pears puts it, 'the structure of reality determines the structure of language'.[11] This is not a tenable position for a poststructuralist, and, interestingly, by the time of the *Philosophical Investigations* Wittgenstein himself reverses his position, suggesting rather that 'our language determines our view of reality, because we see things through it'.[12] This is much closer to the position adopted by Forrest-Thomson, who in effect uses the words of the earlier text to support the later view: that is she uses the same words, but in a different language-game. Towards the close of 'It Doesn't Matter about Mantrippe', the final poem of *Language-Games*, and with characteristic humour – many of her poems are either very funny or have their comic moments, something particularly apparent when hearing her read – Forrest-Thomson plays with Wittgenstein's insights, summed up in the notes for *Solstice* and *Language-Games* as 'basically what we do with our words is what we do with our experience of living' (CP 261):

> People who were here before Wittgenstein came
> still have command of their 'Faculties'.

There are no unacceptable sentences, only
impossible worlds

(CP 47)[13]

Many of the poems written about this time, most of which are
included in *Language-Games*, owe an obvious debt to Wittgen-
stein, and some, like 'The Brown Book' and 'Zettel', acknow-
ledge this at the end of the poetic text, carefully cordoned off
from the poem by brackets. Two of her poems use footnotes as a
device, in each case incorporating material from Wittgenstein. In
particular 'Ducks & Rabbits' uses the 'duck-rabbit' figure taken
from Wittgenstein's discussion of this in the *Philosophical
Investigations*, a figure which Forrest-Thomson also knew from
Ernst Gombrich's classic *Art and Illusion*, to which she refers in
an essay on Empson called 'Rational Artifice'.[14] Wittgenstein
used this figure to explore what he called 'seeing as', because the
duck-rabbit figure 'can be seen as a rabbit's head or as a duck's'
(Wittgenstein1, 194). Wittgenstein suggests through his use of
the duck-rabbit that things can be seen differently according to
the interpretation placed on them, though they themselves may
have not changed. And he makes a distinction 'between the
"continuous seeing" of an aspect' and what he calls 'the
"dawning" of an aspect' (a discussion taken up in Forrest-
Thomson's footnotes to 'Ducks & Rabbits'), for he realizes that it
would have been possible for him to have been shown the figure
and only ever have seen a rabbit. Or, indeed, a duck. This also
introduces the possibility that our initial reading of a figure or a
poem can obscure what else it might be possible to see: hence
Forrest-Thomson's theoretical campaign against premature
naturalization, and her incorporation of poetic techniques
which impede the process of naturalization.

For Gombrich, the most important feature of the duck-rabbit is
how it illustrates 'the problem of convincing representation, the
problem of illusion in art'. For, he points out, although we can
oscillate between the two aspects of the figure, even remember
the existence of the one while looking at the other, 'we cannot
experience alternative readings at the same time. Illusion, we will
find, is hard to describe or analyze, for though we may be
intellectually aware of the fact that any given experience *must* be
an illusion, we cannot, strictly speaking, watch ourselves having
an illusion.'[15] Now you see it, now you don't.

DUCKS & RABBITS
in the stream;[1]
look, the duck-rabbits swim between.
The Mill Race
at Granta Place
tosses them from form to form,
dissolving bodies in the spume.

Given A and see[2]
find be[3]
(look at you, don't look at me)[4]
Given B, see A and C.
that's what metaphor[5]
is for.

Date and place
in the expression of a face[6]
provide the frame
for an instinct to rename,[7]
to try to hold apart
Gestalt and Art.

[1]   Of consciousness
[2]   The expression of a change of aspect is the expression of a new
      perception.
[3]   And at the same time of the perception's being unchanged.
[4]   Do not ask yourself 'How does it work with me?' Ask 'What do I
      know about someone else?'
[5]   Here it is useful to introduce the idea of a picture-object.
[6]   A child can talk to picture-men or picture-animals. It can treat them
      as it treats dolls.
[7]   Hence the flashing of an aspect on us seems half visual experience,
      half thought.

(CP 22)

This is no simple transcription of a scene, though the
'experience of being in a particular place, Cambridge' (CP 261)
was expressly significant to her writing at the time, and the Mill
Race at Granta Place is a well-known Cambridge location,
complete with pub. There ducks do swim to and fro, and after a
drink or two they might well seem to be half-dissolving in the
foam of the rushing water. What makes this different from
Romantic and equally delirious invocations of scenes and birds
is not just the oddity of the metaphorical duck-rabbits, for

Forrest-Thomson is challenging conventional expectations of poetry. The problem is, as she says in *Poetic Artifice*, that 'most people do prefer art to mirror life and... poetry doesn't' (*PA* 81); though if a poet wants to preserve intelligibility as well as make that challenge to conventional expectations in an effort to 'recreat[e] the world through language', she cannot 'forever avoid our attempts to make it do so. Delaying tactics are its only resource'. Here these tactics include the footnotes to the poem.

The main text can be read with or without the interpolation of the footnotes, a choice we are given when reading any academic work, whose validity is conventionally underpinned by this device. (Is this one of the 'academic questions'?) It is certainly difficult to resist the urge to look at the footnote at the end of the first line, so we do tend to include that line of text in the reading, and when we do, the even flow of the rhythm is disrupted, particularly where rhythm is marked by rhyme or assonance. Is this another form of naturalization, this habituation to a scholarly textual convention? The problem of how – literally – to read this poem actually begins earlier than this, with the title itself. Is it part of the poem? Both syntax and punctuation suggest that it is, and that we are therefore being encouraged to regard whatever is on the page as part of the poem. But it is for the reader to decide exactly how, and how also to retain the multiplicity of reference, the shifting perspective that the use of the duck-rabbit image propounds. The fact that it is almost impossible to have it both ways, as we cannot entirely forget the alternate possibility when looking at it in one way, seems to support both Wittgenstein's and Gombrich's analyses of the duck-rabbit schema. And yet something does change; and what changes is our perception.

The duck-rabbit is a trope of perception Forrest-Thomson uses in this important poem about metaphor and the field of vision to engage with the problem of representation: that the human mind, and art, do not mirror reality, but rather represent it according to unconscious or partially conscious conventions. Hence the duck-rabbits are placed in the stream 'of conscious-ness', with a doubling of meaning: for 'stream of consciousness' itself is an important device of literary modernism's challenge to realism's pretensions to reproduce 'reality' or experience. More than an illustration of either art historical or philosophical argument, the poem sets up a duck-rabbit relationship between two possible readings of 'Ducks & Rabbits'. Forrest-Thomson's rejection of synthesis and the deliberate awkwardness and ambivalence of articulation between the two 'halves' of the poem – 'body' of poem and 'footnotes' – provides for the reader a verbal transcription of the visual experience. This is a performative construction in which the oscillation between the two elements – and the twin contexts of philosophy and poetry – generates the necessary tension for the solution of the puzzle that is 'Ducks & Rabbits'. Because 'the meaning' cannot be readily assumed, the reader has to carefully work through the poem to a thematic synthesis, which is the climax to an accumulation and working through of what Forrest-Thomson calls 'image-complexes': a special kind of metaphor of which the duck-rabbit in this poem provides a paradigm. Metaphor is one of the most characteristic features of poetry, and itself involves 'seeing as': seeing something as something else.

The image-complex, another hyphenated concept, clearly owes something to Ezra Pound's famous definition of the 'Image' as 'that which presents an intellectual and emotional complex in an instant of time.'[16] In 'The Separate Planet' Forrest-Thomson defines her term:

> as the traditional rhetorical trope or metaphor ... 'image' because the words used supply the critic with an image – not of course solely or even primarily, visual – of the non-verbal world; 'complex' because these images are juxtaposed one with another in a complex of thought, feeling, evocation, of sense impressions, which the critic must sort out without destroying its complexity. (SP 4)

And the problem for the reader or critic is of course precisely to keep as many as possible of the plurality of denotations, connotations, and associated emotions in play *within* the text rather than looking outside the poem. Which may be why, when she discusses the image-complex again in *Poetic Artifice*, she describes rather than defines it. This also suggests a desire to distance her coinage from the implications of an Imagist collapse of mediation into immediate experience, or 'direct treatment of the "thing"'.

In her preface to *Poetic Artifice* Forrest-Thomson gives a typically rather complex description of how the image-complex functions: it is, she writes, 'a level of coherence which helps us to assimilate features of various kinds, to distinguish the relevant from the irrelevant, and to control the importation of external contexts' (*PA* xii). It is then a *contextualized* metaphor, on the model of Wittgenstein's contextualization of specific words within the language-game in which they are used. And it functions as what Bernstein, developing Forrest-Thomson's ideas, calls an 'anti-absorptive/technique...used toward absorptive ends' (Bernstein, 22), which delimits the potentially endless proliferation of ambiguities while it hinders premature, external naturalization, and integrates different aspects or levels of language in the poem. Through the accumulation of the image-complexes that create the metaphorical level of the poem, 'Ducks & Rabbits' can be made to yield up both an unarticulated image, and a split-off emotional charge. The original split can then be sutured in the experience of the reader, a reader who is envisaged as active in the construction of the text, rather than a passive consumer of the poet's 'vision'.

The image-complex of the duck-rabbit, at once verbal and visual, connects the beginning of the poem with the reference to the theory of Gestalt which forms part of its conclusion:

> Gestalt psychology argues that the human mind does not perceive things in the world as unrelated bits and pieces, but as *configurations* of elements, themes, or meaningful, organised wholes. Individual items look different in different contexts, and even within a single field of vision they will be interpreted according to whether they are seen as 'figure' or 'ground'. These approaches...have insisted that the perceiver is active and not passive in the act of perception. In the case of the famous duck-rabbit puzzle, only the perceiver can decide how to orient the configuration of lines. Is it a duck looking left, or a rabbit looking right?[17]

Raman Selden's succinct summation of Gestalt psychology uses the duck-rabbit figure to explain this concept of the active role of the reader, whose participation in the production of the text has since become a fetishized component of linguistically investigative poetics, but which – far from being routine – was a quite new academic question when Forrest-Thomson was writing 'Ducks & Rabbits'.

References to the theories of metaphor (including those Selden indicates, 'figure and ground', and vehicle and tenor) are drawn out by 'the perceiver' in the search for the thematic synthesis of 'Ducks & Rabbits', which is elaborated in the last stanza. We work through Forrest-Thomson's argument by image-complexes from the duck-rabbits half dissolving in the stream of consciousness set up in verse one, to their analogue in ideas of metaphorical structure in verse two (by reference to that form of metaphor Aristotle identifies as analogy, on the model A:B as C:D). Then we arrive at the enigma of the third stanza. This offers not only a reframing of metaphor, called here the 'instinct to rename', but also a hidden message. Past the memory of an experience captured in the first verse, and its revision in the second, we arrive at an originary experience and image, which though never spoken subtends the whole poem. The subject or thematic synthesis of 'Ducks & Rabbits', for which the rest is a metaphorical transference delineating precisely 'how to orient the configuration of lines', hinted at by the use of 'frame', is now revealed by the lines 'Date and place/ in the expression of a face': it is a photograph.

The sense of intolerable loss and longing released by this perception, the textual equivalent of an eidetic image – and a photograph, whether of self or other, like the child's perception of itself in the mirror, is frozen – is of the very essence of desire. And Lacan specifically identifies the experience of reflection at the Mirror Stage as a *Gestalt*, moreover a *Gestalt* which is a projection: that is it offers an illusion. In 'Ducks & Rabbits' the powerful affect or emotion with which the image – and in this case quite literally the photographic image as well as the poetic – was cathected or invested has been split off by the techniques of artifice. The perceptive split is engineered by language, which divides the 'I' which speaks from the 'I' that is spoken of, subject from object. Image and emotion (and of course feeling is one possible philosophical ground of a non-linguistic reality) are held apart until the final line, which joins what the poem tries with all its craft until then 'to hold apart': Gestalt and Art. The organized whole that is a *Gestalt* – or a poem – is greater than the sum of its parts, and a perception itself is such a *Gestalt*: Forrest-Thomson's performative poem of perception articulates the relation between Gestalt and Art, being and representation. As with 'The Hyphen', the thematic synthesis or 'design of the whole' produced by a reading attentive to all the linguistic elements and forms in this poem exceeds both affectively and intellectually the subject implied by the title. Not only has 'the impossibility of expressing some non-linguistic reality' been circumvented by this remarkable transformation of experience into art; the language-game of philosophy has been transformed by its imbrication with the language-game of poetry into precisely what Wittgenstein explicitly excludes from his philosophy: the category of the aesthetic.

Forrest-Thomson's apparently cerebral poems take extraordinary emotional risks in their artful manipulations of language. The theme of the apparent impossibility of non-linguistic experience appropriated from Wittgenstein, and what happens then to feeling, is central to her work at this time, and is explored further in 'Zettel' (CP 23–5). Zettel is the German for a 'slip' – that is of paper, though the implication of a slippage of language is irresistible to Anglophones – or a 'note', and the Wittgenstein text of that name was edited from a collection of slips and fragments of manuscript and cut-up typescript left in a box file. This method of composition (like Sappho's fragments) has obvious attractions for a poet who works with juxtaposed fragments of other texts.

Forrest-Thomson's transposition in her 'Zettel' of elements of philosophical speculation into the language-game of poetry can constitute the enlarging of our awareness of language and hence also of our capacity for experience that she suggests is possible in her Note to Language-Games. Quoting a philosopher of language lays claim to a particular tradition of what she calls '"pure" intellectual activity', and she explores the relationship between intellectual and other less formal attempts 'to make sense of concrete experience', by juxtaposing fragments of the former – frequently attributed so that we cannot mistake the intention – with snatches of conversation or party settings:

> Anyone who does not understand
> why we talk about these things
> must feel what we say to be mere trifling,
> thus:
> 'It seems a bit of a fuss about nothing.'
>   (she said...

                                            (CP 24)

In 'Zettel' these juxtapositions frequently work to increase the sense of irony, indeed the growing tendency to parody in her work, since the last statement is of course a colloquial reiteration of her quotation in the first three lines of an observation of Wittgenstein's (Wittgenstein2, 34:197). Significantly his remark (in parentheses in *Zettel*) follows a discussion of another form of picture puzzle than the duck-rabbit, and one which hinges on the eventual perception of form in what 'at first glance...appears to us as a jumble of meaningless lines'. He goes on to ask, as indeed we might about 'Ducks & Rabbits': 'what does it amount to to say that after the solution the picture means something to us, whereas it meant nothing before?' Wittgenstein and Forrest-Thomson both prefer to pose such 'academic' questions rather than to answer them: indeed to attempt to answer this one is in large part the entire business of aesthetics. In the case of 'Ducks & Rabbits' I think Forrest-Thomson got it magnificently right, when she said that such a poem can 'form the definition, or affirmation, in time and language, of human identity' (*CP* 263).

'Zettel' includes adaptation and relocations of further statements from Wittgenstein's text, and I will explore a few of these to gather an increased understanding of what might be at stake in Forrest-Thomson's process. Take:

> The concept of a living being
> has the same indeterminacy
> as that of a language.
> Love is not a feeling.
> Love is put to the test
> – the *grammatical* test.
>
> (*CP* 24)

Wittgenstein's words are: 'The concept of a living being has the same indeterminacy as that of a language' (Wittgenstein2, 59:326); and 'Love is not a feeling. Love is put to the test' (Wittgenstein2, 88:504). Even though the words and their order are identical in both cases, in Forrest-Thomson's poem their combination, the setting in which they are embedded, and poetic lineation change their status. As isolated fragments, prior to collection and editing, they form part of 'the language-game of information' (Wittgenstein2, 27:160). Now, taken from the language-game of philosophy they are transformed into the language-game of poetry, undergoing in the process their own grammatical testing of their place in the system of language. Forrest-Thomson suggests in *Poetic Artifice*, as part of her exploration there of the differences between poetic and other forms of language, that when a section of prose is rearranged as verse, the use of poetic artifice alone is sufficient to change 'expectations, modes of attention, and interpretive strategies' with regard to the lexical units, without requiring 'any alteration of the linguistic material itself' (*PA* 22). Fully aware of the materiality of language, she focuses on what Watten describes as 'language as a material for the construction of poetry rather than as a medium for communication'.[18]

The full Wittgenstein text of the second quotation used by Forrest-Thomson is the memorable:

> Love is not a feeling. Love is put to the test, pain not. One does not say: 'That was not true pain, or it would not have gone off so quickly'. (Wittgenstein2, 88:504)

Feeling has already been identified as a possible philosophical ground of a non-linguistic reality, and affect is the product of the earliest manifestations of the drives before the differentiation of consciousness from the unconscious. Forrest-Thomson's other poetic citation of Wittgenstein on pain in 'The Brown Book': 'trying to get between pain and its expression' (*CP* 21), also draws attention to the missing link of non-linguistic reality that can be detected behind Wittgenstein's handling of the subject of pain, and his elision of the distinction between affect and sensation. Forrest-Thomson's own omission – of pain, the correlative that Wittgenstein uses to test love's status as a feeling – is remarkable in a poem that offers so powerfully what Raitt calls the 'extraordinary pleasure ... of a licence to rest in a barely-controlled distress' (Raitt, 305), where the capacity for control is a correlative of the capacity for the exquisite control of the use of language. What is withheld from conscious expression is conspicuous by its absence, like the photograph in 'Ducks & Rabbits'. And the unconscious is another possible source of non-linguistic experience, in unconscious phantasy.

The particular mixing of memory with desire involved in such elaborate reworkings and recontextualizations of material constitutes an investigation of the inner limits of our language and of its leading edge in verbal art, and hence perhaps, as Wittgenstein also suggested, even the limits of our world. This amounts at times, in Forrest-Thomson's work, both poetry and poetics, to the production of an erotics of language, and later, in

Artifice of Absorption, Bernstein will also record the erotics of what he terms 'absorption & repellency' (Bernstein 62), the full and the empty. In Forrest-Thomson's work the erotics of language are focused on melancholy: it is an erotics of pain, and in her later work at times of violence, both linguistic and affective, which is essentially narcissistic, self-reflexive. Bernstein astutely observes that 'the most absorbing possible/ human experience' is that of excruciating pain:

> Excruciating pain obliterates all self-
> consciousness by capturing
> one's entire attention...

> (Bernstein, 47)

Self-consciousness, Bernstein suggests, personal identity, is paradoxically obliterated by the *total* focus on self induced by the experience of an extremity of pain, whether physical or psychological.

In *Zettel* Wittgenstein himself discusses experience in the context of writing: 'The experience of getting to know a new experience. E.g. in writing. When does one say one has become acquainted with a new experience? How does one use such a proposition?' (Wittgenstein2, 101:585). A few lines later, Wittgenstein writes, in a new 'stanza' addressing the voluntary yet 'automatic' movement of writing: 'One's hand writes; it does not write because one wills, but one wills what it writes' (Wittgenstein2, 101:586). In her 'Zettel' Forrest-Thomson's transformation of Wittgenstein's extraordinarily insightful language-game of philosophy into that of poetry creates a subtle and exact representation of the complex and paradoxical relationship between intentionality, consciousness, and the forces of the unconscious in the performativity of writing poetry:

> One's hand writes
> it does not write because one wills
> but one wills
> what it writes.

> (CP 25)

This, the conclusion to 'Zettel', inscribes her response to Wittgenstein in a further example of the transformation of experience into the art of language: precisely the 'compromise between freedom and remembrance' that Roland Barthes, whose work is beginning to influence hers in her thesis, identifies in his early work *Writing Degree Zero* as 'writing' itself.[19]

The poems of the *Language-Games* period which substantially ventriloquate Wittgenstein take material from the language-game of philosophy to produce a new language-game of poetry which can combine with increasing linguistic innovation the traditional techniques and concerns of poetic artifice. Forrest-Thomson's procedural concern with the transformation of experience into art and the intertextual nature of that transformation are evident in her argument that the poem thus produced 'constitutes a new articulation, or experience of life...but of an experience of the life of various forms of language' (PK 64). The only possible articulations of subjectivity and experience are those made through various forms and registers of language. Forrest-Thomson's refusal to make a sharp distinction between criticism and its object, poetics and poetry, by arguing and demonstrating theory in the body of the poems marks the poststructuralist beginning of what becomes a postmodern rejection of the bifurcation of literature into theory and practice. This move is later echoed and amplified in Bernstein's long poem of poetics *Artifice of Absorption*.

Forrest-Thomson is working out an articulation – in both senses – of the theoretical ideas inherited from earlier twentieth-century literary criticism and poetry, a philosophy of language derived from Wittgenstein, and poststructuralist thought. Their integration or hybridization in her work of this period develops and increases in confidence through the period of composition of the poems in her final collection *On the Periphery*, and through the writing of *Poetic Artifice*.

3

On the Periphery

In those days intellectual history was going very fast.

(Roland Barthes)

On the best battlefields
No dead bodies

(Veronica Forrest-Thomson, 'Lemon and Rosemary')

The title of Forrest-Thomson's final and posthumously published collection is plurally resonant. The periphery is the liminal area, the crossover point between two sites, states or places. It is both frontier and boundary, depending on how one is positioned. Being on the periphery is perilously near to being close to the edge. Such liminalities, suggestive and rich in potential, are particularly poignant in the light of our retrospective awareness of how close to the end of Forrest-Thomson's life these poems were written. The periphery is a location that can permit the twilight and the transgressive, one which could indeed be called a 'no-man's-land', and so we might expect an increasing focus on issues of gender. A periphery is a limit and yet permeable at the same time: a poem, however semantically intransigent, can never make a truly hermetic seal between itself and the reader, and it would be a very odd poem indeed that sought to be utterly impermeable rather than simply to resist recuperation. In this respect the periphery invites comparison with another borderline, that between consciousness and the unconscious, especially when we recall Forrest-Thomson's note in *Language-Games* that 'the construction of poems' – here the syntax permits us to read this doubled, as both 'the activity of constructing poems', and 'the form of poems' – records '*thresholds* of the experience of being conscious' (*CP* 263, my emphasis). We can trace how the process of writing itself

43

becomes increasingly the focus, in a way that will be taken up and developed by the Language writers.

Like *Language-Games, On the Periphery* had a precursor volume; in the slender Omens Poetry Pamphlet entitled *Cordelia or 'A poem should not mean but be'* (1974) are ten of the poems also published in her last collection. And in the brief untitled preface to *Cordelia* we find the first clue to the development of Forrest-Thomson's poetic practice, in what appears to be a quotation from the author (who had a fondness for referring to herself in the third person):

> she is 'working on the non-meaningful levels of language which it is poetry's job to bring to the reader's attention, thus providing a link with the past of poetic form and a vision of imaginative possibilities in the future.' (C. 1)

This work, then, occupies the periphery between the traditional and the innovative, and, I would suggest, between a modernist and a postmodernist aesthetic, between Anglo-American literary criticism and theory and that of continental Europe. In particular Forrest-Thomson's writing during this period demonstrates her intellectual engagement with the work of Roland Barthes and of the *Tel Quel* group, who published in the avant-garde journal of that name, including Jacques Derrida. Most important amongst these is the work of Julia Kristeva, whose project followed and in some ways displaced that of her eminent and admiring precursor, Barthes. 'In those days', as Barthes remarked, 'intellectual history was going very fast'.[1]

In his early and 'high structuralist' essays Barthes makes a sharp distinction between criticism and its object: 'criticism is a discourse upon a discourse; it is a second language, or a *metalanguage* (as the logicians would say), which operates on a first language (or *language object*)' (Barthes1, 258). This division between the two language-games is one which postmodern writing questions and subverts, and in an early engagement with his work in her thesis, Forrest-Thomson seizes on Barthes's later concept of *écriture* as the bridge between what she calls 'creative literature' (PK 32) and criticism (which she identifies as 'the interrogation of language by language' (PK 31)) rather than on the concepts of language and metalanguage. 'Barthes provides for this assimilation of criticism by creative literature, or rather, for the amalgamation of the two, by his notion of "*écriture*" which will supersede the particular genres of the poet.' (PK 32) This poststructuralist theoretical move very much reflects her own poetic practice.

Barthes's concept of *écriture* depends on an understanding of writing as an intransitive activity. Rather than conceiving of a writing which is about something and leads to something else – moving between words and world – Barthes posits the existence of a writer, or rather author, *écrivain* rather than *écrivant*, whose focus and field is the activity of writing itself. This emphasis on the process of writing rather than on writing as an object to be interpreted, and on the construction of a poetics of writing, is also evident in the work of the Language writers.

Barthes shares with Wittgenstein a markedly aphoristic style, which lends itself particularly well to a project like Forrest-Thomson's, which borrows words from other contexts. The tension between the movement towards closure – a major feature of the aphoristic style – in the original context and the fracture of that closure in the new language-game of Forrest-Thomson's poems, not only draws attention to the essential ambiguity of language (her interest in which is part of the legacy of Empson), but forms part of that aspect of her project which focuses on the allegedly 'nonsemantic' features of language, as described in the preface to *Cordelia*. The disruption of closure effected by the transposition of a statement from one context to another (without necessarily altering the statement in any way), is a technique which draws on a 'non-meaningful' linguistic practice, in Forrest-Thomson's sense. That is, as Wittgenstein would have understood, it is the context alone which changes the meaning or significance of a statement, as in her use of Archibald MacLeish's concluding lines from 'Ars Poetica',[2] 'A poem should not mean/ But be' as the ironic alternative title of her most ambitious and accomplished poem, 'Cordelia or "A poem should not mean but be"'. 'The process of metaphor,' she says in her thesis, 'regarded as a juxtaposition of language-contexts, is the nearest that poetry may get to the incorporation of extra-linguistic experience' (PK 65): language pushed to its limits, in poetry (as indeed in psychoanalysis) will always attempt to exceed the limitations inherent in its construction.

In her citations of the work of writers like Barthes, Forrest-

Thomson is still pursuing the project of poetry as knowledge outlined in her thesis and in the notes to her various collections. The way the relationship between the cognitive and emotional aspects of knowledge (a subject inherited from I. A. Richards, like her interest in the relationship between science and poetry) appears in different forms of discourse is explored in her thesis. Her own resolution of Richards's problematic split between them is through the structure of the poem, as in 'Ducks & Rabbits', rather than by reference to an external context. That these are more than 'academic questions' is evident in the extraordinary emotional impact of her apparently cerebral poems, though in the thesis the issues are analysed in academic language. This is appropriate enough, but one has to wonder about the considerable defensive potential of the academic register of language. And we might, on the same grounds, question the intellectualism of this poetry, which plays for such high emotional stakes.

> It comes down to saying that the epistemological status of a statement in poetry does not depend on its correspondence with non-linguistic reality; that the knowledge exhibited in a poem is knowledge of certain forms of language and ways in which they can be brought together. (PK 6)

Knowledge, then, is always *of* language, *in* language, and this is how in her poems 'questions of knowledge become questions of technique', of how language is used (CP 262). The new relations Forrest-Thomson engineers between the different areas of discourse juxtaposed in the poems are one of the ways she tries 'to make sense of concrete experience' (CP 262) in her work through forms of knowledge, poetic and philosophical. Knowledge, thus assimilated to experience, then becomes a question of the manipulation of meaning through the techniques of poetic artifice. If experience is constructed through forms of language, then a new articulation is isomorphic with a new experience. This view offers a theoretical basis for the socio-political projects of contemporary linguistically innovative poets in Britain and the United States, including the Language poets, who attempt through their writings not just the breakdown of existing conventions but the inauguration of new perceptions, new possible forms of life.

The assimilation of knowledge to experience evident in Forrest-Thomson's writing also invokes the question of memory, and not just the memory of the individual subject, but that of language itself. Language inevitably retains the impression of its prior usage in any 'new' context. Barthes's enviably elegant articulation of a similar perspective on intertextual relationships, language and writing, in *Writing Degree Zero* also introduces the idea of second-order signification; second-order in that it is based on a previous usage:

> writing still remains full of the recollection of previous usage, for language is never innocent: words have a second-order memory which mysteriously persists in the midst of new meanings. Writing is precisely this compromise between freedom and remembrance.[3]

The tension between this 'freedom and remembrance' is a significant part of both the pleasure of poetry and its status as epistemology, and provides for us at least two levels of intertextual relations: allusions, quotations, and citations (the sources of which are identifiable), and the resonances which all elements of language carry from cultural usage. When words are transposed from one situation to another, say from the language-game of linguistic philosophy to that of poetry, what Wittgenstein called 'the language-game of giving information', that is of communication, provides the link between the two (Wittgenstein2, 27:160). Even at this level, stripped of the context which dictates their interpretation, the words are saturated with cultural meanings, both denotative and connotative, this last the source of metaphor. Indeed it is the memory of language that constructs the very possibility of the existence of poetic language: language at its most highly organized.

Barthes's efforts to deconstruct the idea that signification can ever be innocent forms an important part of his analysis of myth, which he also designates as a 'second-order' system. He acknowledges the problem of 'naturalization' – of such concern to Forrest-Thomson's poetics – as early as September 1956, in 'Myth Today', identifying naturalization as 'the essential function of myth' (Barthes2, 131). Barthes's celebrated cultural poetics essays in *Mythologies* culminate in the discussion in 'Myth Today' of the ideological mystifications constructed by a *Paris-Match* photograph of a young black soldier in French

47

uniform, saluting. Mystifications or mythologizations that can be used to justify colonialism are unmasked – denaturalized – by the application of semiotic analysis, which can deconstruct the metalanguage of myth. Barthes's analysis of myth, especially that in another essay, 'Wine and Milk' (Barthes2, 58–61), feeds directly into Forrest-Thomson's poetry in her 'Drinks with a Mythologue', where Forrest-Thomson plays with the theme of first- and second-order meaning. An earlier version of the poem, as Barnett notes, was entitled 'Drinks with a Metalogue' (*CP* 275), and the change of title marks the movement from a structuralist to a poststructuralist position, by her rejection of the structuralist view of critical writing as inherently metalinguistic.

The dialectic between the first- and second-order meaning, or myth, of wine – in France 'a totem drink' (Barthes2, 58) whose 'goodness' is axiomatic – creates a tension mirrored in the typography that begins to split the two elements of the poem apart:

DRINKS WITH A MYTHOLOGUE

Le vin est objectivement bon   mais la bonté du vin
est un mythe. The veins are obviously bloodless
but the blood in the veins   is mine. A vision
of ordinary beauty resembles the v in the mind.
The v is obvious in but.   It makes beauty
in verbs a myth. Vacillations of opening blood
burst the beauty of v   that is mine. V
in an ordinary bottle   is the breakdown of verbs
in the mind. Violent   and opening beauty, the bursting
of verbs is a myth. Violence objective and but
is this beauty of   veins in the mind.

'If you smash that glass, my dear, you know
you'll simply have to sweep it up again afterwards.
And anyway it's a waste of good wine!'

(*CP* 64)

Forrest-Thomson takes the theme of 'Wine and Milk' as her point of departure for a piece of writing in which the chain of associations, chain of signifiers jerk or flow across a tiny fissure created at the centre of the main body of the poem by the typography, a split occasionally sutured by the second, fourth, sixth and tenth lines, before the coda of the last three lines. This quite modest but destabilizing typographical effect neatly mimes the gap between the signifier and the signified implicit in signification, and, by the way in which this gap slides and closes down the length of the poem, it also mimes what Lacan called 'the incessant sliding of the signified under the signifier'.[4]

The lines establishing this poem are a quotation from the conclusion of Barthes's 'Myth Today' (Barthes2, 158).[5] They are also an abstract of the argument of his 'Wine and Milk' as it relates to the totemic quality of wine for the French, and the multiplicity of significations which this 'substance' can support, creating the 'myth' of the goodness of wine: 'like all resilient totems, wine supports a varied mythology which does not trouble about contradictions' (Barthes2, 58). Wine *qua* wine, as a 'thirst-quenching' drink establishes the first order meaning: 'Le vin est objectivement bon'; the hypostatization of wine carries the second-order meaning or myth: 'In its red form, it has blood, the dense and vital fluid, as a very old hypostasis' (Barthes2, 58).

Barthes ends his argument with a sudden swerve from the semiotic to the political, from tolerant and urbane analysis to sharp ideological critique, when he concludes that 'the mythology of wine can in fact help us to understand the usual ambiguity of our daily life' (Barthes2, 61). For:

> it is true that wine is a good and fine substance, but it is no less true that its production is deeply involved in French capitalism, whether it is that of the private distillers or that of the big settlers in Algeria who impose on the Muslims, on the very land of which they have been dispossessed, a crop of which they have no need, while they lack even bread. There are thus very engaging myths which are however not innocent. And the characteristic of our current alienation is precisely that wine cannot be an unalloyedly blissful substance, except if we wrongfully forget that it is also the product of an expropriation. (Barthes2, 61)

In this case the myth of the essential goodness of wine proves to be just that, a myth, as Barthes unmasks the ideological constructions which permit the perpetuation of this particular mythology. Barthes's political – the evils of colonialism, as also seen in the photograph of the young soldier – becomes Forrest-Thomson's inter- and intra-personal, perhaps through her reading in his allusion to 'our current alienation' a gesture in the direction of the decentred or 'split' subject, as well as to the operations of myth. For alienation is a concomitant both of mystification and of the status of the poststructuralist subject, alienated in language.

As Culler succinctly explains, an inevitable concurrence of what he calls 'the pursuit of signs' (Culler2, vi) is that 'the subject is deprived of his role as a source of meaning. I know a language, certainly, but since I need a linguist to tell me what it is that I know, the status and nature of the "I" which knows is called into question' (Culler2, 33). Similarly, we have learnt to call into question the status of the 'I' set up by a poem. In 'Drinks with a Mythologue' there are at least two possible subjects. The first is the implied 'I' whose thoughts and associations form the main body of the poem. The second is the 'I' whose comments set within quotation marks form the coda of the poem, an 'I' who directly addresses a 'you' who is implicitly the thinking subject, speaking subject of the first eleven lines.

Barthes's epitome of his argument opens the poem: 'Le vin est objectivement bon   mais la bonté du vin/ est un mythe', where the line break strategically isolates 'la bonté du vin' from its declension in 'est un mythe', which the break also serves to highlight. The linguistic, semiotic argument is abstracted from its political context, only to be re-embedded in a context which is deeply and specifically personal, as demonstrated by the last three lines. These conclude the poem on a note of personal (and perhaps gendered) rather than colonial patronage, in the tone of superiority conveyed by the choice of words: 'my dear' and 'simply'; and by signalling ironic distance through the use of the white space, and by quotation marks.

The affective content of the earlier poems is predominantly pain, distress, grief: affects that she describes bittersweetly in 'I have a little nut tree' as 'a silver anguish/ And a golden tear' (*CP* 99). In *On the Periphery* these are increasingly joined, though never supplanted, by rage and anger. 'Drinks with a Mythologue' marks the entry of violence, semantic and semiotic, into Forrest-Thomson's work. It is a sonnet of passion, but of violence, rather than love: 'violent' and 'violence' appear explicitly, as well as 'burst', 'breakdown', 'bursting' and 'smash'. The violence inherent in the colonial and capitalist implications of wine production, the effortless assumption of superiority in the 'voice' of the 'speaker' of the last three lines, breaks through in the use of language and typography in this poem. In 'S/Z' we will also see this violence rupture the surface of the poem in the shock of her translation of Balzac's 'fêtes tumultueuses' as 'violent parties' (CP 112).

The violence that is imaged in the typographic splitting of 'Drinks with a Mythologue' is not simply a semantic violence, but also a violence at the level of the signifier. There are some hints of this in the earlier poems, both intellectually and materially in the text. There is anger in 'The Sentence' (from Identi-kit) a poem framed by its invocation of Caliban, Shakespeare's archetypal dispossessed subject: it begins 'You taught me language' and ends 'but now, at least, I know how to curse' (CP 218). And there is textual violence in her acid use of the pun, of wordplay and of parody, as in 'Grapes for Grasshoppers'.

While not a particularly accomplished poem, 'Grapes for Grasshoppers' is worth pausing on. It opens with a parody of Frances Cornford's 'To A Fat Lady Seen From the Train: Triolet': 'Why do you walk through the world in gloves/ Oh fat white lady whom nobody loves?' In Cornford's rather nastily mysogynist verse the woman (Forrest-Thomson adroitly substitutes 'lady') is symbolically insulated from experience of the world of nature by her formal wearing of gloves:

> O why do you walk through the fields in gloves,
> Missing so much and so much
> O fat white woman whom nobody loves,
> Why do you walk through the fields in gloves...[6]

Forrest-Thomson's poem continues as a collection of proverbial mixed metaphors about the difficulty of writing, where frustration is the dominant theme, including:

> I can't throw stones from castles in air
> or send smoke signals without a fire.
> I must join in writing on this side of the wall.

> (CP 235)

Set in its poetic context this line evokes both the Saussurean comparison of the relationship between signifier and signified to the two sides of a piece of paper (the paper on which one writes), and the sense of confinement within the prisonhouse of language, only able to write on one side – the inside – of the wall. This insulation from direct contact with the world touches the same poignancy aimed at by the Cornford poem, though with the double freight of irony. For we know that direct contact with experience cannot be made textually, except through the mediation of language:

> Why do you walk through the world in gloves
> Oh fat white lady whom nobody loves?
>
> I'm looking for gift horses in the grass,
> hack press or piebald ideas with pass-
> words to let me in to this pretty kettle of vipers.

(CP 235)

I'm looking for clues in puns, twisted words, language-games. In *Poetic Artifice* Forrest-Thomson draws attention to the fact that 'line-spacing across the page...signal[s] the importance of phrases' in poetry without regular metre (*PA* 24), and here we have 'pass-words', where an already idiosyncratic hyphenation is given further emphasis by the line break. The suggestion is of words to pass with, and to pass on – perhaps in both senses: words which will 'let me in', rather than out, since there can be no outside of language in a world created in language. This poem not only foreshadows Forrest-Thomson's later technique of complex parodic citation and quotation, but also and more importantly the thematic synthesis of 'Pastoral', a poem which she calls the 'turning point' of *On the Periphery* (*CP* 264), whose theme is the insulation from experience by language. In 'Pastoral', she says, she was able to realise in practice what she had 'long known in theory': the vital importance for poetry of 'the non-meaningful aspects of language'.

While typographical splitting of the kind found in 'Drinks with a Mythologue' also appears in earlier work, often with a more extreme dislocation as in 'Variations from Sappho', it is in her mature work that the frustration and restlessness that permeate nearly all the poems comes through into the expression of rage, and of violence. The 'v' of 'vin' mutates in a chain of associations beginning with that hypostasis of red wine, blood, carried in 'the veins'. The indication given by the initial French sentence that Forrest-Thomson's reading of *Mythologies* was in French is reinforced by the reference to 'V/ in an ordinary bottle': *vin ordinaire*. But with wine the genie in the bottle – from a different kind of myth – is frequently let out. Inhibitions are released, restraints on behaviour 'breakdown', proverbially truth can come out (*in vino veritas*); the power of the contents of an ordinary bottle can be extraordinary:

V

in an ordinary bottle   is the breakdown of verbs
in the mind. Violent   and opening beauty, the bursting
of verbs is a myth.

Even the capacity for articulation can be lost in this verbal breakdown. 'V', or 'v', is the signifier, while 'the v in the mind' is at once the signified, the mental image or conceptual meaning of 'v', and also V for Veronica, as she often signed herself. Susan Howe will later make similar use of and play on 'sh',[7] at once the injunction to be quiet and the initials of her own name – and of a progressively more radical typographic dislocation than Forrest-Thomson's. It is in 'Three Proper' from *Language-Games* that Forrest-Thomson first makes an implied identification of her forename with the initial 'V': 'And V had better mind her p's/ *and* q's' (*CP* 38). But we should bear in mind that for Forrest-Thomson, the poet in the text, like the reader, and like all the 'I's and 'You's the poem constructs, is always a fiction (*PA* 69). 'V' can also represent the cleavage between the two hemispheres of the cerebral cortex: 'the v in the mind', which like the two elements of the poem, separated by a gap, is also sutured at points, like words joined by a hyphen.

The obscurity of some of the lines takes considerable decoding, and of course a total recuperation is neither possible nor desirable since, to paraphrase Bernstein, the poem written in any other way is not the poem (Bernstein, 11). One of the apparently simpler sentences is 'The v is obvious in but', where of course it is not 'obvious' in the usual sense at all. In early printing and writing, 'u' is frequently rendered as 'v'. But we have also learnt, as in 'Sappho', to remember the resemblance of the written 'u' to the spoken 'You'. The 'v', the cleavage or split (implying duplicitousness) in 'You', then, is obvious in the word 'but' which you (the interlocutor who speaks the coda) use. And 'but' conveniently alliterates with the range of other 'b' words (bon, bonté, blood, beauty) matching the proliferation of 'v' words in the poem, and setting up a phonic – both 'b' and 'v' are labials – and visual pattern as part of the 'non-meaningful' level of language in the poem.

Some of the more obscure statements involve paradox. In the line 'The veins are obviously bloodless' the mimicry of the syntax and first letters of 'Le vin est objectivement bon' partially explains the substitution, as a metaphor for the alleged arbitrariness or lack of motivation of the signifier, since we might find 'The veins are apparently bloodless' more physio- logically accurate. However 'objectivement', for which 'ob- viously' substitutes, also carries the implication of 'from the outside'. But while the 'bonté' apparently carried in the wine is a myth, the blood that is actually carried in the veins is not a myth. It is not a matter of ideology but of actual possession, known to the 'I' by a more intimate means of perception than the visual. However, it is in looking from vin to veins that the correspondence between them is acknowledged, and the capacity both possess of flowing – or more violently 'bursting' – out of their containers.

'Vacillations of opening blood' images the slitting of the wrists; 'opening' the wrists was the ancient Roman suicide of choice, and 'V' is also the Roman figure 5. Empson has a poem 'Letter V', where 'V' stands for five; a poem of deceived love: 'You are a metaphor and they are lies/ Or there true least where their knot chance unfurls'.[8] In Forrest-Thomson's thesis she gives a clever reading of Empson's poem based on the scientific metaphors, but by doing so misses – consciously or uncon- sciously – the affective heart of the poem (PK 292–303). In Empson's 'Letter V' the letter sent contains lies, and the poem ends with the hope that its lines may 'invert to points' – like the letter 'v' itself – and transfix the sender: 'Cross you on painless arrows to the wall'. This subtle allusion to Empson helps us towards an interpretation of the intense sense of deceit, pain and rage in the poem that coalesces around all the 'v's, and is undercut by the last three lines.

In the tiny but vivid drama of this poem, the scene staged in language is of a movement between inside and outside, between stream of consciousness and verbalization. An inner monologue is shot through with elements taken from an obviously heated discussion or row, of which we are only in possession of the interior of one side. This brief passage of inner 'free' association actually follows clearly signalled paths of signification, of metonymic substitution, in which plural identifications of v,

54

wine, blood, language and myth break into consciousness. Then, apparently after the 'I' set up by the first section of the poem threatens to smash a glass of the wine that is the physical accompaniment to the metaphysical debate, the 'scene' ends outside. And it ends with the condescending remarks of the 'You' the poem has constructed, giving us by implication an indication of the inner state of the second 'subject'. This offers one level of naturalization of the poem.

On another level, the phrase 'drinks with a mythologue' tells a tale of drinking with someone who tells stories. The stories we call myths put a particular spin on things, when what is at stake – like the implication of wine in France's atrocious colonial history – may be very different. 'I'm being told stories' then easily becomes 'I'm being told lies'. The text refers to 'the breakdown of verbs in the mind', where the syntax allows the double reading of breakdown as analysis, as well as disintegration, of that part of language which is used to designate action or being. The other is then caught deceiving the I, hence the rage, which is too powerful for a disagreement about the status of language, however passionate. While this 'good wine' is certainly being drunk (or spilt, and perhaps the indication is that it is no more worth crying over than the proverbial milk), in the metaphysical company of the Barthes of *Mythologies*, the textual Barthes of 'Wine and Milk', it would be a mistake to identify Barthes as the interlocutor of the poem: it is undoubtedly the very personal here which is the political.

The importance of Barthes's poetics, a poetics of the always already written, to her work of this period is further demonstrated in a poem Forrest-Thomson read on 17 April 1975 at the Cambridge Poetry Festival, but which was – unlike the other five she read that day – not included in *On the Periphery*. 'S/Z' is named for the text in which Barthes introduced the influential concepts of the readerly and writerly text. Barthes's project in this structuralist *tour de force* (poised on the very brink of poststructuralism) was to create an index of the cultural codes, accumulations of cultural knowledge, intertextual discourse, through which a text becomes intelligible. It is through familiarity with manipulating these codes that the reader becomes active in the construction of the meaning of the text. Hence Barthes's *S/Z* is paradigmatic of the importance of the reader as producer of the text. This is equally of significance to Forrest-Thomson and her successors, though it is worth mentioning by way of a caution how easily these innovations can themselves become a new orthodoxy and thus lose their force. The difference between the *lisible* and *scriptible*, the readerly and writerly text – which has considerable significance for the development of Language writing – is that while the readerly text offers the 'consumer' readily assimilable meaning, is apt for immediate naturalization or absorption, the writerly text requires the work of the no-longer-passive reader to produce from among the plurality of possibilities an open play of meaning. This has profound consequences for the construction of subjectivity:

> *I read the text.* This statement...is not always true. The more plural the text, the less it is written before I read it. .... I is not an innocent subject, anterior to the text, one which will subsequently deal with the text as it would an object to dismantle or a site to occupy. This 'I' which approaches the text is already itself a plurality of other texts, of codes which are infinite or, more precisely, lost (whose origin is lost)... Subjectivity is a plenary image, with which I may be thought to encumber the text, but whose deceptive plenitude is merely the wake of all the codes which constitute me, so that my subjectivity has ultimately the generality of stereotypes. (Barthes3, 10)

The idea of a subjectivity of stereotypes is clearly particularly engaging for a poet who had already written (in 'Sagittarius') that 'a blueprint is no guarantee/ against anonymity', and called her first collection *Identi-kit*.

In *S/Z* we have the dazzling spectacle of an assumedly readerly text in the realist tradition progressively transformed into a writerly text. In a virtuoso performance of immaculate detail, Barthes disrupts the process of naturalization by disclosing the codes which permit its operation. In his analysis of Balzac's novella *Sarrasine*, Barthes breaks the text down into fragments which he calls 'lexias', a process which he calls 'starring' the text 'instead of assembling it':

> We shall therefore star the text, separating, in the manner of a minor earthquake, the blocks of signification of which reading grasps only the smooth surface, imperceptibly soldered by the movement of sentences, the flowing discourse of narration, the 'naturalness' of ordinary language. (Barthes3, 13)

Fragmentation will increase the dissociation between the lexias and defamiliarize the process of reading which unconciously integrates or naturalizes the codes. For example, the phrase 'one of those daydreams' which appears in *Sarrasine* implies that this kind of daydream is all too familiar to the reader. But is it familiar from lived experience, or from previous experience of reading? Forrest-Thomson takes this element of the daydream from Barthes's analysis to 'star' in her poem. 'Au fêtes tumultueueses:/ rêveries profondes' is (even if we correct, the presumably unintentional, grammatical error to *Aux*) a combination of the different versions of Barthes and Balzac. Barthes selects '*À fêtes tumultueuses, rêveries profondes*' for analysis (*S/Z* 25 – my emphasis), saying that Balzac's whole phrase 'is a conversion of what might easily be a real proverb: "*Tumultuous parties: deep daydreams.*" The statement is made in a collective and anonymous voice originating in traditional human experience' (Barthes3, 18), rather, that is, than in the voice of 'an author'. While the original text actually reads: '*au sein des fêtes les plus tumultueuses*' (my emphasis).[9] Forrest-Thomson, whose fondness for the proverbial we have already noted, takes similar freedoms with her 'originals', including a change from plural to singular, 'saisissent' being replaced by the less grammatical 'saissit' (itself presumably a misspelling for 'saisit') and her textually disruptive alteration of the translation from the formality of the original.[10] The turbulent force that in her work drives language to an extreme, often just short of the 'outer limit, impermeability' in its desire for escape from the 'inner limit, absorption'(Bernstein, 48) – as Bernstein paraphrases Zukofsky in *Artifice of Absorption* – is rendered material here in her extraordinary translation of 'tumultueuses' as 'violent'; another verbal and structural correlative of the affective content of violence in her poems.

Like Wittgenstein, the Barthes of *S/Z* takes nothing for granted; his is an exhaustive line-by-line analysis of the text, always enquiring why exactly this is being said, why here, in what manner, and to what effect; discovering how meaning is textually constructed. The kind of attention paid to each word, each lexia, is intriguingly more like the attention customarily paid to the placing of each unit of language in the analysis of poetry. And as with Wittgenstein, elements can be removed, recontextualized, turned to whatever end Forrest-Thomson requires. Though the title of *Sarrasine* is Barthes's first lexia, reminding us of Forrest-Thomson's similar manoeuvre in 'Ducks & Rabbits', in her 'S/Z' she chooses the first sentence as her opening stanza:

S/Z

J'étais plongé dans une de ces
rêveries profondes
qui saissit tout le monde
même un homme frivole
au sein des fêtes les plus tumultueuses.

Au fêtes tumultueuses:
rêveries profondes.

I was sunk in one of those
profound daydreams
which grab everyone
even a trivial man
in the middle of the most violent parties.

At violent parties:
profound daydreams.

That is one of the rules Balzac uses
and Barthes notices.
There are many other rules,
but I don't want to mention them.
We can – some of us – sometimes
forget the whole problem.
I mean the only problem:
What is true.
I write no question mark
after that question.

There are a few answers, such as:
Literature matters.
What else is there.
What am I going to do with my life.
Write another book, I suppose.
What else is there.
I expect no answer.

Poems teach one that much:
to expect no answer.
But keep on asking questions;

that is important.
Just hope the house doesn't fall down
for I have no insurance.

Je suis plongée dans une de ces
rêveries profondes
qui saissit tout le monde
même une femme frivole
au sein des fêtes tumultueuses.

                                    (CP 112–13)

The plot of Balzac's *Sarrasine* turns on the eponymous hero's misrecognition of a castrato for a woman, which has tragic consequences, and gender is equally significant in Barthes's analysis. Forrest-Thomson's only and elliptical allusion to this theme of the uncertainty of sexual difference lies in the change of gender in her final stanza from 'un homme frivole' to 'une femme frivole', a move by which the woman poet appropriates the male novelist's words in a recapitulation of the opening of both poem and novel. This change of gender is an ironic mirroring of Barthes's analysis of the first lexia:

> The title raises a question: *What is Sarrasine?* A noun? A name? A thing? A man? A woman?... The word *Sarrasine* has an additional connotation, that of femininity, which will be obvious to any French-speaking person, since that language automatically takes the final 'e' as a specifically feminine linguistic property, particularly in the case of a proper name whose masculine form (*Sarrazin*) exists in French onomastics. Femininity (connoted) is a signifier which will occur in several places in the text; it is a shifting element which can combine with other similar elements to create characters, ambiances, shapes and symbols. (Barthes3, 17)

Barthes's explanation of his looking-glass formula 'S/Z' (Sarrasine slash Zambinella) in lexia XLVII is worth quoting in full to get the baroque flavour of his writing, beside which Forrest-Thomson's language seems a model of economy. His argument turns on the question of castration: physical in the case of La Zambinella, in the cause of his art; psychological in the case of the sculptor Sarrasine, who uses cutting tools in his own art.

> *SarraSine*: customary French onomastics would lead us to expect *SarraZine*: on its way to the subject's patronymic, the Z has encountered some pitfall. Z is the letter of mutilation: phonetically, Z stings like a chastising lash, an avenging insect; graphically,

59

cast slantwise by the hand across the blank regularity of the page, amid the curves of the alphabet, like an oblique and illicit blade, it cuts, slashes, or, as we say in French, *zebras*; from a Balzacian viewpoint, this Z (which appears in Balzac's name) is the letter of deviation (see the story Z. *Marcas*); finally, here, Z is the first letter of La Zambinella, the initial of castration, so that by this orthographical error committed in the middle of his name, in the center of his body, Sarrasine receives the Zambinellan Z in its true sense – the wound of deficiency. Further S and Z are in a relation of graphological inversion: the same letter seen from the other side of the mirror: Sarrasine contemplates in La Zambinella his own castration. Hence the slash (/) confronting the S of SarraSine and the Z of Zambinella has a panic function: it is the slash of censure, the surface of the mirror, the wall of hallucination, the verge of antithesis, the abstraction of limit, the obliquity of the signifier, the index of the paradigm, hence of meaning. (Barthes3, 106–7)

The slash also recalls the barred subject of Lacanian theory, $, symbolic of the split or decentred subject, of the lack of being at the heart of subjectivity. Barthes's textual performativity, drawing attention to the materiality of language, is evocative of Forrest-Thomson's own interest in the 'phonological/visual level' of language, (*PA* xiii) as in 'Drinks with a Mythologue'. In the crescendo of the final piling up of phrases Barthes fills the sign 'S/Z' with sense, reference and meaning, in contradiction to his avowed desire for a language emptied of these (a desire which is part of the reason why Barthes avoids writing on poetry, since poetry seems inevitably saturated with meaning).

> The man who wants to write must know that he is beginning a long concubinage with a language which is always *previous*. The writer does not 'wrest' speech from silence... but inversely, and how much more arduously, more cruelly and less gloriously, detaches a second language from the slime of primary languages afforded him by the world, history, his existence, in short by an intelligibility which pre-exists him, for he comes into a world full of language... We often hear it said that it is the task of art to *express the inexpressible*; it is the contrary which must be said (with no intention of paradox): the whole task of art is to *unexpress the expressible*, to kidnap from the world's language, which is the poor and powerful language of the passions, another speech, an exact speech. (Barthes1, xvii–xviii)

His fantasy of this speech seems to be, as Culler remarks, a language 'light and clean, not weighed down or filled with meaning'.[11] The very opposite of his language in *S/Z*. This makes Forrest-Thomson's subversion of Barthes's rhetorical excesses with her own prosaic, even laconic, statements all the more interesting. Particularly when we come to her observation of what can be missed if one is carried away by one's own rhetoric, as Barthes seems to be, in this obsessive form of textual close analysis:

> We can – some of us – sometimes
> forget the whole problem.
> I mean the only problem:
> What is true.

The lack of a question mark emphasizes the rhetorical nature of the question, which is also indicated by the flatness of the affect. In the Cambridge reading, her emphasis falls on 'only' – 'the *only* problem' – to underscore that this is not just the heart of the matter but the all and sum. The next three questions are also shorn of the conventional and expected punctuation: 'What else is there.' 'What am I going to do with my life.' 'What else is there.' The rules are there, the rules of structure that 'Barthes notices', or rather constructs through his identification of them; the rules of grammar and of punctuation; but in poetry those rules can be subverted or even dispensed with altogether.

> Poems teach one that much:
> to expect no answer.
> But keep on asking questions;
> that is important.

This focuses us again on poetry as epistemology, recalling Wallace Stevens's 'One goes on asking questions' in 'The Ultimate Poem is Abstract'; and it is worth remarking that both Forrest-Thomson and Culler cite Stevens in texts they were apparently writing around the same time, and where there are other intertextual relations.[12]

'Just hope the house doesn't fall down/ for I have no insurance' in this context is reminiscent of Forrest-Thomson's lines in 'The Lady of Shalott: Ode' from *On the Periphery*, which also talk about truth and literary convention in terms of bricks and mortar:

> And estate-agents must beware;
> For if what we are seeking is not the truth

And we've only a lie to share,
The modern conveniences won't last out,
Bear tear flair dare,
And the old ones just don't care.

(CP 86)

'The house' is also obviously the house of literature, 'for I have no insurance' – that is nothing to fall back on – nothing 'to do with my life' other than to write another book. (Are the estate-agents then the literary critics?) 'What else is there./ I expect no answer.' These statements do not require an autobiographical reading, though of course they teasingly invite just that.[13] The 'I' of the poem, as we know, is a construct. In 'S/Z' these statements could as easily be a ventriloquization of Barthes, or a stereotype of 'the writer', for one thing is certain: the 'I' of this poem is literary, and primarily a writing, rather than a speaking, subject. There is also an intertextual echo of the conclusion to Empson's essay 'Obscurity and Annotation', in which he is at pains to set aside arguments against innovative forms of poetic analysis: 'Certainly all new acts are dangerous, but it is not necessarily less dangerous to avoid them. I may be run over if I go into the street, but the roof may fall on me if I stay indoors.'[14]

That the house of literature, and of poetry as emblematic of literature, is in a state of – potentially dangerous – disrepair, is an issue that preoccupies Forrest-Thomson. In the *Collected Poems*, Barnett has with nice discrimination placed 'S/Z' after 'Richard II'. For 'Richard II', which was written for inclusion in the event (and later appeared in the book) *Poems for Shakespeare*,[15] deals with precisely the issue of the condition of the house of poetry, which is 'on the periphery' between the conservation of poetic tradition and the possibilities of renovation offered by new techniques. Here these new techniques are epitomized by the mutating refrain of temporal deictics, which are usually used to anchor utterances in time, and are here set loose at the end of stanzas one ('Forever again before after and always'), four ('Again before forever after and always'), and seven ('Before forever after again and always'). In the stanzas that make up the poem, recapitulations of earlier poetic techniques of rhythm, rhyme, alliteration are intercut with an exploratory tour of a decaying home/poem,[16] imitating the language of a surveyor's report: 'This reading would be accounted for by the very damp condition of the building'. The poem ends with a 'dangerous act', performed on the very roof of that house. An act which attests to Forrest-Thomson's belief about the future of poetry, and the potential for artifice of what she called 'non-meaningful levels of language' (PA xiv) in the detached, floating, unmotivated, unpunctuated final line:

> In the joinery timbers there is new infestation
> And a damp-proof course is urgently needed.
> Say a few prayers to the copper wire.
> Technicians are placing flowers in the guttering
> They are welding the roof to a patch of sky
> Whatever you do, do not climb on the roof.
> Before forever after again and always.
>
> limpid eyelid
>
> (CP 111)

The materiality of language and poetry are compared to the materiality of experience, but in a material world in which we can envisage a surreal welding of the roof to the sky. A world in which forever, before, after and again can shift the temporal sequence in which they appear, though they will always end with an elegiac and insistent 'and always', for Forrest-Thomson's poem is set against the final section of Richard II's final soliloquy, on the theme of time.[17] The performativity of her poetry is superbly in evidence in this meditation on a soliloquy which begins with Richard seeking to 'compare/ This prison, where I live, unto the world', as Forrest-Thomson seeks to 'compare' the prisonhouse of language with the external world. And in the course of Richard's speech he describes the setting of 'the Word itself/ Against the Word';[18] a most potent image for the activity of a poststructuralist poetics.

In her writings of this period Forrest-Thomson continues the development of a poststructuralist perspective on language and its possibilities begun while at Cambridge. Her increasingly self- and language-conscious writing demonstrates the free play and plurality of signification inherent in the potentially infinite recession of meaning which Derrida celebrated in his landmark lecture at Johns Hopkins University in 1967, which, at a conference intended to introduce structuralism to North America, inaugurated deconstruction.[19] The rejection of closure which *différance* implies, Forrest-Thomson performatively constructs at the 'conclusion' of 'On Reading Mr. Melville's *Tales*': 'the differment remains, remains and' (*CP* 68). As Forrest-Thomson writes in 'Address to the Reader, from Pevensey Sluice' (*CP* 65), where meaning and the avant-garde or innovative text are concerned:

> If it were quicksand you could sink;
> something needing a light touch
> soon and so simply takes its revenge.

We are well advised to bear this in mind if captured by the acutely personal twist in the tale that the most accomplished of her poems have, like the poignancy of the photograph in 'Ducks & Rabbits', the elegiac refusal of closure of 'Richard II', the coda of 'Drinks with a Mythologue', or the final shift of gender at the conclusion of 'S/Z'. In 'Address to the Reader' there is another such, which moves between the theoretical and the personal in describing the relationship between 'the reader and his writer' in ironically sexual terms. It is worth noting here, in the light of the delicate and ambiguous negotiations with gendered subjectivity which appear in Forrest-Thomson's poetry, that there is always a distanciation, to ward off naturalization, and avoid biographical or 'confessional' resonance.

> Follow the reader and his writer,
> those emblematic persons
> along their mythic route
> charting its uncertain curves and camber;
> for to be true to any other you must –
> and I shall never now – recover
> a popular manoeuvre known mostly as,
> turn over
> and go to sleep.

> (*CP* 65)

Here we are distanced from the subjective through the device of 'the reader and his writer'. Having followed Barthes's analysis of these figures' respective roles and 'mythic route', it becomes impossible to 'be true' to any other, any previous account of such relationship, to return to a traditional model of intercourse. Barnett notes that a version of this poem first appeared in *Earth Ship* no. 12, which bore the subtitle: 'A Womens Issue' (*CP* 275).

And the conclusion of the poem – notoriously a woman's accusation against an inattentive male sexual partner after climax – is a traditional 'popular manoeuvre' frequently experienced as signifying rejection. To be 'true', faithful, to the canonical trajectory of poetry and poetics, it would be necessary – and now impossible – to reject the seductive possibilities of poststructuralist thought.

In 'Address to the Reader' Forrest-Thomson metaphorically registers 'the undertow of all those trips/ across to France', those trips of the mind I am discussing here, imaged through the materiality of actual landscape and journey. And they are indeed trips, or excursions, that Forrest-Thomson made. For she preserves throughout her sense of the validity and significance of traditional poetry and poetic techniques, and is concerned with retaining and 'providing a link with the past of poetic form', rather than, like Kristeva, emigrating.

4

Poetic Artifice

One strong help for the pastoral convention was the tradition, coming down from the origin of our romantic love-poetry in the troubadours... that the proper moments to dramatize in a love-affair are those when the lover is in despair.

(William Empson, *Some Versions of Pastoral*)

He: ...It is all up with the once bindingly valid conventions, which guaranteed the freedom of play.
I: A man could know that and recognize freedom above and beyond all critique. He could heighten the play, by playing with forms out of which, as he well knew, life has disappeared.
He: I know, I know. Parody. It might be fun, if it were not so melancholy in its aristocratic nihilism.

(Thomas Mann, *Doctor Faustus*)

No poet lived more completely in literature yet managed to inscribe the pain of existence so sharply on allusive verse.

(Peter Porter)[1]

In the innovative poetry of the twentieth century, and especially in the writing which characterizes the end of that century and the beginning of the new one, it is clear that we can no longer rely on a particular register of language to signal the difference between poetry and prose. This makes what Gérard Genette calls the 'poetic disposition',[2] which is revealed in the ordering of lexical units on the page, and in their relationship to the white space, an extremely important ground of difference. As Forrest-Thomson says,

> Poetry can only be a valid and valuable activity when we recognise the value of the artifice which makes it different from prose. Indeed it is only through artifice that poetry can challenge our ordinary linguistic orderings of the world, make us question the way we make

sense of things, and induce us to consider its alternative linguistic orders as a new way of viewing the world. (*PA* xi)

The possibility of these 'alternative linguistic orders' depends upon the existence of established orders and codes of language, such as those analysed by Barthes. They depend, that is, upon what – following Kristeva – we might think of as the inherently intertextual disposition of written language.

Chapter one of *Poetic Artifice*, 'Continuity in Language', begins with Forrest-Thomson's recognition of the fact that in poetry one is playing with the tensions between ordinary and extraordinary uses of language: 'language is common both to the realm of poetry and to the domain of ordinary experience, and this is one of the main factors with which a study of poetic language must deal' (*PA* 18). And it is upon ordinary language, she says, the language which provides us with the non-verbal world 'of emotions, objects and states of affairs', that poetic 'Artifice must work to create its alternative imaginary orders'. In her essay 'Irrationality and Artifice', another of her texts which uses 'Artifice' in the title, Forrest-Thomson connects her 'argument to the claim made by Julia Kristeva [a claim founded on the work of Jakobson] that poetic language is an exploitation of the processes of giving sense that underly all the other, more restricted, kinds of discourse' (IA 124). The argument is that poetic language is not just reliant on its interrogation of the structural aspects of other forms of language, but relies on our understanding of its variance from those structures, and therefore the intertextual relationships between them.

Kristeva's work is important for reading Forrest-Thomson's for two reasons. The first is Kristeva's own engagement with the subject of poetic language, a preoccupation of Forrest-Thomson's own poetics; and the second, which is unquestionably the more important, is the concept of intertextuality. Forrest-Thomson never discusses intertextuality as such, though her entire poetic *oeuvre* could be said to be founded on her own intuition of intertextuality, a concept which is susceptible of two interpretations. The first is often considered to be that which Kristeva 'intended', and as defined by Leon Roudiez (the editor of *Desire in Language*, citing a definition given by Kristeva in *Revolution in Poetic Language*), is 'the transposition of one or more *systems* of signs into another', and has 'nothing to do', he asserts, 'with matters of influence by one writer upon another, or with the sources of a literary work' (Kristeva, 15).[3] That is, the network of allusion, citation, quotation from other discourses which make up any text are not attributable to a specific source, but rather to forms of discourse themselves. The second, rather more permissive reading of intertextual relationships, includes those works in which the fabric of other preconstructed texts incorporated in the 'new' text can be attributed to other sources, either identifiable or half-recalled. In spite of Roudiez's strictures, in practice Kristeva's discussions of intertextual relations move between these two poles.[4] Intertextuality, then, includes not only what Culler calls 'the general discursive space that makes a text intelligible' (Culler2, 106), but also the system of textual relations between different discourses, and between different individual texts.

In Forrest-Thomson's use of Wittgenstein the transposition of units of language from the language-game of philosophy into the language game of poetry involves what might be called both the generic and the specific forms of intertextuality, while in her textually performative 'Drinks with a Mythologue', there is a more diffuse incorporation of, or intertextual relation with, Barthes's concept of myth and the essay 'Wine and Milk'. The question of a range of possible intertextual relationships is important for Forrest-Thomson's later work because of the development in her poetry from a late modernist preoccupation with fragmentation to a parodic textual citation which is poised on the verge of a postmodern articulation of intertextuality.

An interest in the intertextual is one of the platforms of the structuralist and poststructuralist revolt against the idea of the autonomy of the text (as asserted by the New Criticism) and the movement – rhetorically if not in practice – from a literary critical focus on interpretation to a focus on structure and systems of relations: that is, from an emphasis on what a text means to how it means. A concomitant of the paradigm shift involved in intertextuality is a renegotiation of the idea of authorship: the birth of the intertextual reader at the cost of the death of the author. Barthes writes in his essay 'The Death of the Author', that 'writing is that neutral, composite, oblique space where our subject slips away, the negative where all identity is lost, starting with the very identity of the body writing'.[5] As Culler puts it, 'the reader becomes the name of the place where the various codes can be located: a virtual site' (Culler2, 38). The focus of critical interest then falls increasingly on writing itself – Barthes's *écriture* – and 'textual analysis', an analysis founded on the concept of intertextuality, comes to replace 'literary criticism'.

Culler's grasp on this is characteristically lucid:

> A text can be read only in relation to other texts, and it is made possible by the codes which animate the discursive space of a culture. The work is a product not of a biographically defined individual about whom information could be accumulated, but of writing itself. To write a poem the author had to take on the character of poet, and it is that semiotic function of poet or writer rather than the biographical function of author which is relevant to discussion of the text. (Culler2, 38)

An interesting paradox, which Culler notes, is that the already-presentness in language of any expression apparently denies the possibility of the shock of the new. However, we know that the force of poetic language lies precisely in its capacity for innovation: particularly in the case of metaphor, as Forrest-Thomson's arresting duck-rabbits demonstrate. And yet, this or any metaphor clearly relies for its intelligibility on pre-existing linguistic conventions. This central paradox necessarily underlies any discussion of intertextuality and linguistic innovation, or the relationship between the traditional and what has been known as the avant-garde. Here we can see one aspect of the destruction of the very conditions of possibility of an avant-garde which characterizes the postmodern, since if the relationship between the form and the meaning of what is written is thus always already present, what possibility can there be for the irruption of an innovatory, revolutionary language-act? The other aspect, the increasing commodification of language in late or globalized capitalist culture, forms an important motive for the writing of the Language poets.

No longer regarded as an 'autonomous' object, the text is now read as a process, and this goes hand in hand with the renegotiation of subjectivity which is so important for Forrest-Thomson's work. Kristeva comes in again here, with her concept (related to that of intertextuality) of the subject in process, in which the play of language in French, '*sujet en procès*' also carries the sense of 'the subject on trial'. That is, the integrity of the subject (previously assumed, like that of the text) is put on trial by the unconscious activity of the drives, and the subject is no longer conceived of as singular and unified, but as split: divided between unconscious and conscious processes.

While the relationship between psychoanalysis and linguistics articulated by Lacan, which is such a vital connection for Kristeva's work here, clearly never had the same direct significance for Forrest-Thomson, aspects of Lacan's work have given so powerful a form to speculations about identity and existence that they have come to be seen as the paradigm for poststructuralist thinking about subjectivity and the problems of identity. In particular Lacan's formulation of the Mirror Stage, his emphasis on desire, his discussions of the split subject, the unconscious as being structured like a language, and the Other, offer powerful tools for the discussion and interpretation of linguistic constructions of subjectivity such as those we find in Forrest-Thomson's poetry.

In an early essay from *Semiotiké* later translated for inclusion in *Desire in Language*, Kristeva underlines the equation of textuality and subjectivity: 'any text is constructed as a mosaic of quotations; any text is the absorption and transformation of another. The notion of *intertextuality* replaces that of intersubjectivity, and poetic language is read as at least *double*' (Kristeva, 66).[6] As Barthes reflects in *S/Z*, 'this 'I' which approaches the text is itself already a plurality of other texts'[7] (Barthes3, 10).

It is indeed, as Culler remarks in connection with the presuppositions implicit in the concept of intertextuality: 'a characteristic experience that one's presuppositions are best revealed by another. They are perhaps that which must be revealed by another, or by an effort of *dédoublement*: of thinking from the point of view of the other' (Culler2, 102). To be a critic of poetry requires the capacity for just such a *dédoublement* or doubling: the ability to work both with the consciousness of the subjective 'I' set up by the poem and with the status of the poem itself as art object; 'not only the *subject's* utterance but the *object* of analysis and critique', as Isobel Armstrong describes it.[8] Culler's correlative for *dédoublement*, 'thinking from the point of view of the other', rather obscures the usual, and in the case of Forrest-Thomson's poem 'Canzon' (*CP* 102–3) more pertinent –

and psychoanalytic – translation of the word: dividing or splitting in two.

CANZON

for British Rail Services

Thou hast committed
fornication

Sols sui qui sai lo sobr'afan qe.m sotz

I know I am not the only to suffer the pains of love.
But this I also know: that each who loves thinks so.
For myself I can only say,
I doubt if any other
Has suffered more than myself
From this overloved desire.

It is always a wrong move
In the chess game of all we do;
It upsets the sparkling play
Whose light desire does smother;
It destroys all kind of breadth
And plunges a quagmire

Myself is at one remove
Because it has gone to you
Who will not display
The sense of me another,
Being bound in yourself
By my forlorn desire.

Everything goes to show
That those are lucky who
Keep themselves away
From tangling with another
Cold and in themselves
Unlike my absurd desire.

I desire to love
You and be loved by you
Who cancel out my play
Being so much another
Being so much yourself
Away from my require.

You check my every move
By being what you will do
And not what I could say

71

To you, my love, an other,
Suffering more myself
By overlove and desire.

And yet I would not not love
If I could choose not to;
For I require to play
By hazarding myself
To you, my self, the other
Whom I always desire.

CODA

For
I am Arnaut who drinks the wind
And hunts the hare from the ox
And swims against the stream.

(CP 102–3)

In this exquisite poem included in both *Cordelia* and *On the Periphery*, Forrest-Thomson finds a way not only of speaking the almost unspeakable – increasingly a characteristic of her intensely self-reflexive work – but also of performing an 'effort of *dédoublement*' in the more usual translation. She perceptively describes the restless, self-defeating strategies of 'forlorn desire':

My self is at one remove
Because it has gone to you
Who will not display
The sense of me another,
Being bound in yourself
By my forlorn desire.

An extraordinary grasp of a range of complex psychoanalytic ideas can be detected in the miracle of compression of these lines, including desire, the split subject and the Mirror Stage, but especially the intricacies of what Melanie Klein called projective identification. This term describes a special mode of projection in which 'the subject inserts his self – in whole or in part – into the object in order to harm, possess or control it.'[9] And projection is always necessarily accompanied by splitting: *dédoublement*. It is worth remembering that in the discourse of psychoanalysis 'the object' refers to another human being, an aspect or part of them, or more frequently to the subject's phantasy of that person, and that projection and introjection are the two most important mechanisms of identification. In this

72

stanza then, the subject's 'self' is projected onto the other, which then fixes or confines the other as a phantasy object: 'Being bound in yourself/ By my forlorn desire'. As such the other cannot be itself, which deprives the speaking subject of the very gratification it seeks, for then the other is unable to reflect 'the sense of me another' – the subject's own otherness, for which in alienation it longs. When the subject seeks its truth in the 'other' rather than the Other, as in 'Gemini', it is inevitably a painful and self-defeating exercise in narcissism, its recurrence part of a repetition compulsion:

> And yet I would not not love
> If I could choose not to;
> For I require to play
> By hazarding myself
> To you, my self, the other
> Whom I always desire.

The doubling under discussion here is also central to the process of internal naturalization which Forrest-Thomson seeks to privilege in *Poetic Artifice*. The very existence of an addressee within the text, and not just the inevitable implied addressee, but an explicit 'you' as well as an 'I' – twin subject positions for the reader to occupy – implies an intertextuality: the existence of a prior discourse. As of course do poems which include questions, like 'Gemini' and 'S/Z', even if the conventional punctuation is removed and 'I write no question mark/ after that question'[10] (*CP* 112).

Dédoublement is, of course, a technique ripe for irony, and as such is used by Shakespeare in the *Sonnets*, where the 'I' of the poem sets up an other to be apostrophized. This irony is exercised notably in Sonnet 94, which Empson subjected to a considerable analysis in *Some Versions of Pastoral*.[11] Forrest-Thomson uses both Shakespeare's sonnet and Empson's reading of it in her introduction to *Poetic Artifice* to present a paradigm for the method of interpretation – suspended naturalization through attention to the techniques of poetic artifice – which she intends to practise and discuss in that text. 'Canzon', ironically and bathetically dedicated 'for British Rail Services',[12] resonates by allusion and citation with that most extraordinary of Shakespeare's sonnets: 'They that have power to hurt and will do none', Sonnet 94, as we shall see.

However, it is not the sonnet form that Forrest-Thomson adopts and adapts in this instance. In 'Canzon', as we might expect from the title, she uses a formal structure based on the Provençal or Occitan *canzone*,[13] the Troubadour lyric of courtly love, one form of which will typically describe love in terms of its pleasurable torments. Forrest-Thomson frequently uses the tension between the expectations aroused by the employment of a classic form and her divergences from it, as well as being concerned to link 'the past of poetic form and a vision of imaginative possibilities in the future' as she explains in her preface to *Cordelia*. Her use of the techniques of and allusion to the poetry of the past is intended to provide a level of linguistic continuity, so that the reader will not get irretrievably lost in that 'exploitation of non-meaningful levels of language' which Forrest-Thomson thought necessary both to 'a vital contemporary poetry', and to 'the future of poetry' (*PA* xiv).

'Canzon' successfully draws together the medieval, the Elizabethan and the contemporary. The form and part of the content quote from the medieval Provençal, but 'Thou hast committed/ fornication' is taken from Marlowe's *The Jew of Malta*,[14] and also forms part of the epigraph for T. S. Eliot's early poem 'Portrait of a Lady' (Eliot1, 18). This textual reference within a textual reference links early modern to modernist writing. The poem's lineage in 'the past of poetic form' can be defined even more precisely: its precursor is in the work of Dante's *il miglior fabbro* of the *Purgatorio*, Arnaut Daniel.[15] Renaissance and contemporary letters are joined again by this intertextual resonance, for it was Dante's compliment to Daniel that Eliot – himself much influenced by Dante – applied to Ezra Pound, who helped him shape the final form of his modernist masterpiece *The Waste Land*, when he dedicated that poem to him. It is a compliment Forrest-Thomson herself transferred to J. H. Prynne in a manuscript annotation to a published version of her 'Pastoral' (*CP* 276). And Renaissance and modern literature and language are also joined by Forrest-Thomson's central extended metaphor of the game of chess, which both Saussure and Wittgenstein use to discuss how language works, and which Eliot takes from Middleton's *Women Beware Women* to title the second section of *The Waste Land*, reinforcing Forrest-Thomson's theme of desire and betrayal: 'Thou hast committed/ fornication'.

74

Forrest-Thomson's main formal modification of Daniel is to exchange his six stanzas of seven lines each for seven stanzas of six lines each, with the insertion of the first three lines which have no correlative in Daniel's *canzone* structure. Perhaps they form an epigraph, since the first two form part of one of Eliot's epigraphs, split to emphasize 'fornication' (Marlowe does this by giving the word to another speaker), and the third is, as we shall see, an approximation of the first line of Daniel's otherwise untitled 'Canzon XV', 'Sols soi qui sai lo sobrafan que.m sors': 'I alone know the great suffering that looms up at me'.[16] Part of the reason for this quotation may be because, as James Wilhelm remarks, this poem in particular was 'cited by Dante as a paragon of stylistic elegance'.[17] In addition, Pound remarks that 'En Arnaut made the first piece of "blank verse" in the seven opening lines of the *Sols sui*'.[18]

The antecedents of 'Canzon' can be even more exactly located, since it seems clear that Forrest-Thomson was acquainted with Daniel through Pound's *Translations*, the basis of which was Canello's edition of Daniel.[19] A version of the original is printed parallel to Pound's translation, and her version 'Sols sui qui sai lo sobr'afan qe.m sotz' is close to Pound's 'Sols sui qui sai lo sobrafan quem sortz', following Canello. The reader without knowledge of Daniel or Old French might be forgiven for reading this line in 'Canzon' as an extreme example of the 'non-meaningful' levels of language. Indeed at one level it operates exactly as that, for, deliberately or not, errors in transcription have crept in which render part of the line 'nonsense' – what Forrest-Thomson prefers to call 'non-meaningful' – to experts.

Forrest-Thomson's poem both echoes and undercuts the statement in Pound's and Daniel's first three lines which cast the speaking subject of the poem as a uniquely suffering lover, and which Wilhelm translates as: 'I am alone the one who knows the overwoe of love/ That soars in a heart suffering from overlove', and Pound archaically renders as 'I only, and who elrische pain support/ Know out love's heart o'r borne by overlove,/ For my desire...'[20] Their highly romantic and narcissistic lines are answered in hers, where the syntax, though decipherable, would be less exact without knowing that of the lines – especially Pound's 'I only' – to which they respond:

> I know I am not the only to suffer the pains of love.
> But this I also know: that each who loves thinks so.

The last line of her first stanza brings together Pound's 'overlove' and 'desire' into 'this overloved desire'. It is tempting to read this undoubtedly ironic compression as a wry commentary on the emphasis on 'desire' which Lacan's rereading of Freud had brought into such critical prominence, and which at the same time is a major theme of this poem. Line endings, and particularly stanza conclusions are always a significant position in poems (another inheritance from 'the past of poetic form'), and 'desire' is repeated with variation at the end of five of the seven stanzas: 'overloved desire', 'forlorn desire', 'absurd desire', 'overlove and desire', and finally straight 'desire', just before the coda.

Sonnet 94 makes its appearance through stanzas four and six (with my italics for emphasis):

> Everything goes to *show*
> That those are lucky who
> Keep themselves away
> From tangling with an*other*
> *Cold* and in *themselves*
> Unlike my absurd desire.
> . . .
> You check my every *move*
> By being what you *will do*
> And *not* what I could say

'Canzon' employs the vocabulary, something of the rhythm, and the chilling tone of Shakespeare's monumental tribute to the pains of love – with nothing pleasurable about them – while using the simplicity of the shorter Provençal lyric line to undercut the grandeur of the sonnet form:

> They that have power to hurt and will do none,
> That do not do the thing they most do show,
> Who, moving others, are themselves as stone,
> Unmovèd, cold, and to temptation slow

The slightness of the verbal grounds for resemblance, yet the undeniability of the allusion demonstrates again how difficult it is in practice to restrict the interpretation of the concept of intertextuality to undifferentiated units of language or to preexistent bodies of discourse. Forrest-Thomson cites the same Shakespeare sonnet in her line 'You choose to do what you do show', from 'In Memoriam', though with a twist to the affirmative. This is another poem of the torment of love: 'Hurting me by slow by slow'[21] (CP 100). 'Canzon' moves between these echoes of lyric power, traditionally markers of poetic language, to a more open and conversational, almost prosaic tone familiar from 'Ducks & Rabbits'. There are also overtones of modernist free verse, in taking the risk of a slight ungainliness which counterpoints the more lyric moments:

> For myself I can only say,
> I doubt if any other
> Has suffered more than myself

While risking the collapse into the commonplace this resistance to melodrama and overstatement at once increases the poignancy of the restless distress of the body of the poem and gives no preparation for the extraordinarily haunting coda, with which 'Canzon' ends:

> For
> I am Arnaut who drinks the wind
> And hunts the hare from the ox
> And swims against the stream.

In this quotation I have preserved the typography of *Cordelia* in preference to that of the *Collected Poems*. It is an almost exact translation of Daniel's *envoi* to 'Canzone X': 'Ab gai so conde e leri', of which Wilhelm says 'These lines are some of the most memorable that Arnaut ever composed'. He translates this stanza as 'I am Arnaut, who hoards the wind/ And chases the rabbit with the ox/ And swims against the swelling tide'.[22] A further comparison of Daniel's original with Pound's translation and Forrest-Thomson's reinscription clearly shows her capacity for lyric mastery, and for something more: that capturing of the affective charge and its release at the conclusion of the poem we saw in 'Ducks & Rabbits':

Arnaut:

> Eu son Arnauz c'amas l'aura
> e chas la lebr'a lo buo
> e nadi contra siberna.[23]

77

Pound:

> I, Arnaut, love the wind, doing
> My hare-hunts on an ox-cart,
> And I swim against the torrent.[24]

Forrest-Thomson:

> For
> I am Arnaut who drinks the wind
> And hunts the hare from the ox
> And swims against the stream.

Pound admits the inadequacy of his translation in a note following his version (the original text does not accompany his translation on this occasion): 'I have translated it badly even if my idiom does mean about the same as the Provençal'.[25] This bears witness to the Italian proverb about the dangers of translation, *traduttore traditore*, to translate is to betray. Forrest-Thomson's version is not only closer to the original – reading *buo* as ox rather than ox-cart – but has significantly greater rhythmic elegance and poetic power.

The difference between Pound's and Forrest-Thomson's versions, and the increase in power hers acquires turns on two moments of the exercise of poetic artifice. The first relies, as do so many of the most powerful moments of her poetry, on her willingness to diverge from her model: it is the metaphor in 'drinks the wind', which has an extra appositeness in the watery context of the final line. The second is that tiny shift from Pound's 'torrent' to Forrest-Thomson's 'stream', making the astute wager of adopting a weaker word to acquire an alliterative capacity that far outweighs the loss of verbal force. An astonishing poignancy is conveyed by these small changes. It is the increasing incidence of such moments of poetic maturity which not only reveal her extraordinary grasp of the potential of artifice, but have the double edge of causing us to mourn the loss of what her work might have become: 'a vision of imaginative possibilities in the future'.

'Poetry maintains the sublime in the old sense', she writes in the final chapter of *Poetic Artifice*, 'Pastoral and Parody', 'by creating the sublime in the new' (*PA* 129). In her view this sublimity is created by giving priority – she calls it 'dominance' – to the 'non-meaningful aspects of language' in the develop-

78

ment of new poetic techniques which can absorb the conventional, formal and social aspects of the past of poetry. This is particularly important for her elaboration of the concepts of pastoral and parody as the central principles of her programme for the future of contemporary poetry, 'the triumph of artifice' (*PA* 146). By way of example, she quotes what 'an Arab writer of the ninth century says of Moorish poetry' concerning the conventional device known as the *kharga*, which is not only 'the nearest equivalent to the Western refrain; it was the model for the Troubador coda':

> it is accounted an imperative rule that the poet, breaking off from the subject matter of the lyric, should pass on to the *kharga* without any transition, and that he should represent it as being uttered by characters who speak in their own names, or, if they remain silent, are connected with a theme other than that of the poem. The *kharga* is frequently couched in childish language or in a foreign tongue. In any case it is a customary convention that it should produce the effect of meaningless jargon. (*PA* 129)[26]

This effect is arguably produced by the Provençal line at the beginning of 'Canzon', and certainly by the final line of 'Richard II'. Most importantly, we see here the origin of the convention by which the coda in Arnaut Daniel's poem of disappointed love is spoken as by an 'I' called 'Arnaut', and why this stanza is entirely adjacent to the content of the rest of the poem. The assertion of poetic identity and the accompanying abrupt disjunction is moving enough in the original, but is enhanced by its fictional relocation in Forrest-Thomson's poem. Affectively, the charge the coda carries is increased by its appropriation for her adaptation of the Occitan form and subject matter, her joining of the past of poetic form to her vision of imaginative possibility. Theoretically it not only provides an example of Ibn Sana al-Mulik's 'imperative rule' for the *kharga*, linking the Moorish practice of the ninth century to that of the Troubadour poet of the late twelfth century, but also provides a link to modernist poetry through the translations of Pound, and with poststructuralist theory (and indeed with the postmodern practice of parodic quotation, with which I will engage later) through Forrest-Thomson. For she discusses this particular feature of artifice in her analysis of Dada, whose heirs in France were the poets and writers associated with *Tel Quel*.

It has been suggested by Heather Glen, a fellow postgraduate who knew Forrest-Thomson well, and was bridesmaid at her wedding to Jonathan Culler, that some of the humour in the poems of this period derives from Forrest-Thomson's ironic address to the theoretical questions which were preoccupying Culler in his own work at the time.[27] Humour there certainly is, which sometimes gets missed by her readers, but not by those who attended her readings. And ironic address to theoretical questions, or more pointedly to the personality cults which arise around theoreticians – 'these saints/ of the new dispensation are haloed/ in self-approbation' (CP 248) – but her own interest in the issues was serious. There are, though, clear correspondences between Culler's *Structuralist Poetics* and *Poetic Artifice*, including references to Wittgenstein, quotations from Wallace Stevens, similarities of phrasing, and concern with naturalization. In a footnote, Culler refers his readers to Forrest-Thomson's discussion of naturalization: 'The best discussion of convention and naturalization in poetry is V. Forrest-Thomson, *Poetic Artifice*' (Culler1, 271, n. 19). Both texts were written at around the same time, at least in part during the period of their marriage (1971–4). *Structuralist Poetics* was published first (in 1975), and although in the bibliography *Poetic Artifice* is cited as being published by Blackwell in 1974 (Culler1, 280), it was not in fact published until 1978, and then by Manchester University Press. These factors suggest an intertextual relationship of time and circumstance that would seem to be very much an effect of 'the "context in which we occur"/ that teaches us our meaning' (as she puts it in her Cambridge poem 'The Hyphen' (CP 35)). This is a special form of the second, wider reading of intertextuality.

Initially Forrest-Thomson saw language as providing a kit of tools for the investigation of identity, and subsequently as the means of constructing subjectivity and experience. Her engagement with the work of the continental theorists involves an increasing recognition of the instability of language and thus of meaning, and an increasing problematization of subjectivity. With 'the death of the author' there can be no central guarantee of meaning such as that provided by the concept of authorial intention. The undecidabilities of signification, founded, according to Saussure, on the arbitrariness (or more accurately the conventional nature) of the relationship between sign and referent, make it impossible to refer to an origin of meaning in the world external to the word, the text. Indeed the argument of *Poetic Artifice* – and much of her poetry of this period – can be regarded as a sustained attack on ideas of reference, and the basis of her argument is the necessity for texts to resist naturalization, narrative assimilation. Resistance to assimilation and to naïve ideas of reference also features prominently in the poetry of the *Tel Quel* poets whom she translated and in the writings of the *Tel Quel* theorists (inevitably often the same figures), as it does in the work of succeeding contemporary innovative poets – like the Language writers – as well as in her own poetry of the period, as 'Pastoral' demonstrates.

PASTORAL

They are our creatures, clover, and they love us
Through the long summer meadows' diesel fumes.
Smooth as their scent and contours clear however
Less than enough to compensate for names.

Jagged are names and not our creatures
Either in kind or movement like the flowers.
Raised voices in a car or by a river
Remind us of the world that is not ours.

Silence in grass and solace in blank verdure
Summon the frightful glare of nouns and nerves.
The gentle foal linguistically wounded
Squeals like a car's brakes
like our twisted words.

(CP 72)

The resistance to immediate explication set up in Forrest-Thomson's poetry creates a build-up of emotional tension, by the repression of what is not, cannot, or will not be spoken, and this then finds its representation by a means other than description or expression. Her handling of naturalization is not only the key to her attempts to capture the relationship between language and reality that we call experience, but also the basis of her readings of the work of other poets, including those whose work is incorporated in her own, whether directly by citation, or as here generically, by invoking the history of 'pastoral' in the title of this poem.

The two key terms of pastoral and parody are introduced in

Poetic Artifice as analytic categories, essentially to replace the outworn form and content. These had become increasingly irrelevant to a poetry in which form becomes content (as Valéry put it, 'What is form for others is subject matter for me'),[28] and content becomes form through the transposition of material from one language-game – increasingly that of the past of poetry itself – into another.

Forrest-Thomson's discussion of the combination of pastoral with parody in the work of poets she respects is her attempt to articulate an aesthetics of, and a future programme for, postmodern linguistically investigative poetry (though it is unlikely that she would have known or used these terms). Pastoral, that long-outmoded genre, is boldly chosen to stand as a metonym for the category of artifice, which is capable of transforming the material of the language-game of communication into the language-game of poetry. Parody stands as a metonym for the technique of incorporating other language-games into the language-game of poetry. Forrest-Thomson credits John Ashbery, Jeremy Prynne, and Sylvia Plath, like Eliot before them, with the rare ability to perform the difficult balancing act of combining the two, unlike Ted Hughes, or 'Messrs. Lowell, Berryman, Gunn, Davie, Larkin, Alvarez, Hobsbaum and Mrs Sexton', whose 'apocalyptic insensitivity' she deplores (*PA* 151).

In the history of literature pastoral is epitomized by sophistication which pretends to natural simplicity – like Marie Antoinette at the Trianon playing at milkmaid – and pastoral poetry dwells, often at length, on the *amours* and distresses of shepherds and shepherdesses in idealized rural landscapes. Empson had already extended the remit of pastoral (for which, interestingly, he claims the work of Gertrude Stein, a strong influence on Language writing),[29] and Forrest-Thomson's use of the term takes off from his definition of 'putting the complex into the simple'.[30] Like parody, pastoral has its origins in classical literature, and is characterized by elaborate artifice.

Forrest-Thomson's own 'Pastoral' fuses the two when it mocks the idealization of the rural by ironic defeats of expectation, like that produced by the bathetic turn of 'Through the long summer meadows' diesel fumes'. Pastoral speaks, as she clearly recognizes, of a 'world that is not ours' in the social as well as the literary historical sense, and at the same time it is a

82

poetic world from which we are estranged by the contemporary loss of acquaintance with artifice. Rural 'creatures' and 'clover' are invaded now by 'raised voices in a car', and the 'gentle foal' in pain 'Squeals like a car's brakes': more urban and mechanical metaphorical invasion. '[O]ur twisted words' have their meanings perverted, are brutally wrenched from their objects, unlike the limpid artifice of the language of dwellers in Arcadia. In 'Pastoral' the maintenance of the conventional levels of formal metre, rhyme, and rhythm allows for a greater degree of abandonment of concern by the poet for the very meaning of the words, let alone the interpretation of the poem as a whole.

In her preface to *On the Periphery* Forrest-Thomson traces what she calls 'the graph of this book' (*CP* 264), or more accurately of the technique of her poems. This trace begins with the 'extreme of aleatory poems', which like her attempts at concrete and sound poetry are soon abandoned, 'and ends, in "The Lady of Shalott", by recapturing the right to speak directly through the traditional ranges of rhymed stanza'. She describes a trajectory through which the development of new techniques can lead the poet to a place in which past, previously exhausted techniques can again become available for use. 'Pastoral' is at the zenith of that curve, where 'what had been tendentious obscurity of meaning becomes, therefore, a tendentious refusal of meaning, except the minimum needed to create verbal form at all'. Forrest-Thomson underestimates, it seems to me, the availability of meaning in this poem, but it is certainly clear that what she calls the 'tendentious obscurity of meaning' of the intermingling of elements of language drawn from different complex discourses of her earlier poems is here replaced by something which is much more akin to Dada: in particular to Dada's technique of 'random' juxtaposition, and the Dadaist rejection of referential meaning.

It is important to draw attention to the levels of meaning in 'Pastoral' that she marginalizes, to interrogate her assertion. For example, in lines like 'Either in kind or movement like the flowers' an echo of Shakespeare's Sonnet 94, which haunts so much of her finest work, persists. And not just in the content, though in the sestet of Sonnet 94 'They that have power to hurt', who are the kind who move others while remaining unmoved, are compared to flowers, and in particular to 'the summer's flower'. It is the form which is the vital structure underpinning an otherwise flimsy intertextual ghost of Shakespeare's poem, through the resonances set up by an identical rhythm and the use of a truncated sonnet structure.

Now follows part of Forrest-Thomson's account of 'Pastoral'; a rare opportunity to see how she perceives her poetics to function in a poem which is so importantly about language and writing:

> If one writes a line like the first line of this poem one is obviously alerting the reader to the fact that sound resemblance – 'clover'/'love' – is more important than meaning. The second line furthers the process in making it clear that the extension of meaning is less important than the way external contexts – the meadow, the flowers, the cars, the voices, the river – feed back into the thematic synthesis which is given in the fourth line and developed through the other two stanzas. This is particularly noticeable in the last two lines, where the 'gentle foal' is important for his *entle oal* sounds rather than for his physical being. For these sounds are taken up in 'linguistically wounded', which is a crucial phrase both for the theme and for the rhythm. That is, the foal's physical being is transferred to the sound of the names we give him. A pretty paradox in view of the poem's theme; since the poet is saying (thematic synthesis) just that: pre-occupation with linguistic problems prevents contact with the physical word. (*PA* 125)

The phonological argument in Forrest-Thomson's work of this period becomes increasingly familiar, as in her Jakobsonian attention to 'our favourite key of *o*' (*PA* 108), but her point about sound resemblance is intriguing. In this poem it is not only phonological but also visual, the twin aspects of the signifier, and interestingly the poem was actually published in 1975 as a visual object, a poster, by the Cambridge Poetry Festival (*CP* 276). But surely the temptation is to ignore or suppress the 'c' of 'clover' and read 'lover', rather than 'love', by visual and phonological assimilation to 'love us'? The poem is certainly enigmatic: we are not told what the 'creatures' are, simply that they belong to and 'love us', whoever the 'we' of this poem, which includes the reader, may be. But whatever the creatures are, whether 'clover' refers to the actual flower, a proper name, or the situation of being 'in clover', all of which resonate around the word, they are lay figures to focus us within the poem on the subject of 'names' and the tyranny of naming, for 'names' are 'not our creatures': clearly a reference to and rejection of Adam's dominion over the beasts by naming them, as well as a rejection of nomenclaturism.

Names are jagged, like the 'day with jagged edges' of 'Sagittarius', not smooth, or organic as 'scent' would indicate. They are jagged, painful, tearing to speak, to write, refusing to fit neatly into place. They are 'not our creatures': rather, we or our experience are theirs, are under their domination.[31] Words, names, used by others – 'raised voices' overheard – remind us of our alienation in language as well as the existence of other figures in the landscape, they 'Remind us of the world that is not ours'. And alienation in language is the inevitable experience of the subject who cannot be self-identical. There are either too many words, an overwhelming profusion of material, or none at all: none, that is, for that which is too painful to be spoken, which is thus forbidden articulation. Like Shakespeare's great Sonnet 94, 'Pastoral' configures an unbearable emotional pain figured in language, and at the simplest level this is the pain inflicted by 'our twisted words'.

What Raitt characterizes as Forrest-Thomson's 'drive to capture the interaction between language and reality' receives confirmation from a circumstance surrounding this poem which so significantly engages with the operations and limitations of language (Raitt, 305). The original typescript for this poem bears an annotation in her own hand: 'my first head-on collision successfully averted', and a sketch of the near-miss car incident.[32] This reinforces the impression of a collision between machine and animal created by the logic of 'The gentle foal linguistically wounded/ squeals like a car's brakes', and the conclusion that the 'squeal like *the* car's brakes' (the variant in *Cordelia* (C. 18); my emphasis) attributed to the 'wounded' foal is drawn from this situation. Perhaps the generalization involved in the change from the definite to the indefinite article is part of an attempt to avoid the temptation to external naturalization. Certainly a similar interpretation can be derived from within the confines of the text, avoiding external in favour of internal naturalization, by following the development of the image-complexes. I remain, though, uneasy with Forrest-Thomson's description of the '*entle oal*' sounds as 'taken up in "linguistically wounded"'. This seems to be one of her occasional over-statements of the case for the significance of the 'non-meaningful' elements of language, detachment of signified from referent.

It is the very physicality of the word that Forrest-Thomson makes apparent in her poetry, the materiality of thought which is her particular gift and signature, which derives in part from her awareness of the materiality of language. At the end of the quotation from *Poetic Artifice* above the simultaneous existence of a barrier between words and world and the slippage between the two is evoked: 'pre-occupation with linguistic problems prevents contact with the physical word'. The urge is to read 'physical world', and close the circle of the inherent paradox.[33] The emotional charge which the theme of the poem contains and insulates – the loss of contact – is an unbearable grief: the pain of 'our twisted words' potentially far greater than that of twisted limbs.

The pleasurably/painfully playful exercise in this poem of the theoretical concerns with language haunting her translations of the *Tel Quel* group and citations of Barthes and Kristeva is, as so frequently in her poems, undercut by her intensely personal though far from 'confessional' sense of the tragedy of identity and experience: that they are dependent upon the frailty and instability of language for their construction, their registration. This is a major feature in the last of the poems from *On the Periphery* I will consider here, 'Sonnet', which is also an exemplar of a particular form of parody, a genre founded on intertextuality.

In *A Theory of Parody* Linda Hutcheon draws attention to the complex range of parodic strategies available to contemporary artists such that 'parody in this century is one of the major modes of formal and thematic construction of texts' (Hutcheon, 2). It functions importantly as a highly contemporary 'mode of self-reflexivity' and as 'one of the ways in which modern artists have managed to come to terms with the weight of the past' (Hutcheon, 29). These are both vital issues to Forrest-Thomson's work, and Hutcheon quotes from *Poetic Artifice* in her argument for the importance of parody to twentieth-century art. She also concludes her introduction by referring to the quotation from Thomas Mann which forms my second epigraph to this chapter.[34] It is from a dialogue between a composer, Leverkuhn (I), and the Devil (He), in which the devil refers to the exhaustion of creativity in the art of music and its replacement by mere technique, so that 'Art becomes critique'. When art becomes critique, that is self-reflexive, does it necessarily become 'uncreative'? Is parody necessarily parasitic and denigrating, as traditional formulations would insist, or can it be symbiotic, energizing? Both Forrest-Thomson and Hutcheon suggest the latter possibility. Parody involves a double movement, or, in Barthesian terms, double coding – Hutcheon calls it, after Bakhtin, 'double-voiced' (Hutcheon, 4) – of conservation and innovation, in which continuity and discontinuity can be held in balance in 'the parodic incorporation that leads to renewal through synthesis' (Hutcheon, 97). This of course is the effect of renewal Forrest-Thomson sought to produce through the incorporation of one language-game in another, keeping continuity and discontinuity in a delicate balance. A postmodern use of parody such as that Forrest-Thomson articulates in her later poems can choose between, and even alternate between, humorous irony and serious tribute, as it negotiates this double part: this textual *dédoublement* in which the juxtaposition of materials from other sources in the language-game of poetry can produce the possibility of a new perception.

Forrest-Thomson's employment of a postmodern parody is frequently 'fun' and playful, but its main feature is that other term of the devil's perceptive analysis of the potential of parody: its essential quality of melancholy. However, it seems to me that the coexistence of humour and melancholy – familiar from medieval literature and most readily from Shakespeare – is a paradox rather than a contradiction. And representation is itself founded on absence or loss. Melancholy is a frequent aspect not only of the content of Forrest-Thomson's poems, particularly the later work, but also of the structure. It is evident both in the employment of a range of references and devices of artifice from the history of poetic language and in the affective charge contained by the poems. The melancholia of parody, then, is my initial theme in discussing 'Sonnet', pre-eminently her 'Artifice' poem, which demonstrates the most refined use of the parodic technique characteristic of her later work. A poem which, more perhaps than any other, exemplifies Forrest-

Thomson's unique capacity for combining the conventional with the formally active, the canonical with linguistically innovative elements of poetry, through her dexterity with the various devices and levels of poetic artifice.

SONNET

My love, if I write a song for you
To that extent you are gone
For, as everyone says, and I know it's true:
We are all always alone.

Never so separate trying to be two
And the busy old fool is right.
To try and finger myself from you
Distinguishes day from night.

If I say 'I love you' we can't but laugh
Since irony knows what we'll say.
If I try to free myself by my craft
You vary as night from day.

So, accept the wish for the deed my dear.
Words were made to prevent us near.

(CP 91)

First poem in *Cordelia*, 'Sonnet' is the final poem of the 'On the Periphery' section of the *Collected Poems*, taken from the text of the typescript Barnett identifies as 'OP 73'. As he points out, the preface to *On the Periphery* designates 'Sonnet' as 'the last poem' (CP 264), though it was included with the group of poems under the heading 'Last Poems' in the published edition. This textual evidence for its final position is also supported by powerful internal claims on the ultimate position in terms of theme and form. As Peter Porter says in his perceptive *Observer* review of *On the Periphery* (12 December 1976), 'there is hardly a line in these poems that does not prompt the question "Where have these words been and what have they brought with them?"' 'Sonnet' is notable for its refinement of artifice and of parodic structure. It recaptures the past by taking for its pattern the most exquisite of verse forms, the archetypal lyric mode of the sonnet. The emphasis on our estrangement in language makes it, like 'Pastoral', both thematically and structurally important in Forrest-Thomson's work.

Poetry can be a memorialization of experience, which

partakes of both psychic or internal, and external reality, and memory and memorialization are connected to Freud's productive preoccupation with the structural relationship between mourning and melancholia in his essay of that title (Freud, XIV, 243–58). My reading of the process I identify in Forrest-Thomson's later poems is intimately connected to my reading of the experience of mourning, and the failures of that experience Freud called melancholia. The melancholic has not mourned the event, the loss, the experience. That which has not been mourned cannot be a memory, though it can be remembered. That rememory (to borrow Toni Morrison's expression), that re-embodiment will be the source of distress and blockage until fully discharged. That which cannot be grieved will inevitably embody itself as a grievance, like a 'foreign body' in the psyche (Freud, II, 139, 165, 290) and recur in psychic life.

Forrest-Thomson's use of preformed language units in quotation of and allusion to previous texts is effectively an articulation of the memory of language as part of the system of language itself. Not only the memory of language, but also the unconscious of language is engaged. Poetry can be, as well as a conscious working through of perception in language, engaged in the representation of unconscious processes through its manipulation of space and units of language. Where the process of citation particularly involves poetic texts, as in the parodic citation developed in Forrest-Thomson's later poetry, what we are dealing with is not simply memory – the eventual outcome of the process of mourning the loss of a loved object – but rather melancholia, where that loss is denied by incorporating the object in the self. Or by incorporating it in an extension of poetic identity, in the subject of the poem.

Melancholia depends upon identification, an identification Freud defines as narcissistic. It becomes entirely self-reflexive rather than continuing to be object-related since the very choice of object for the melancholic is always narcissistic (Freud, XIV, 249). Freud expresses the distinction between narcissistic and hysterical identification in terms of cathexis, or attachment of affect, and withdrawal of cathexis:

> The difference ... between narcissistic and hysterical identification may be seen in this: that, whereas in the former the object-cathexis is

abandoned, in the latter it persists and manifests its influence...
identification is the expression of there being something in common,
which may signify love. Narcissistic identification is the older of the
two... (Freud, xiv, 250)

We have seen that the question of the motility of the affective
charge involved in identification – 'which may signify love' – is
important for Forrest-Thomson's poetry, and I have already
cited Raitt's perceptive remark that for Forrest-Thomson
'theories of poetry are also beliefs about identity' (Raitt, 307),
that is of psychic functioning, of the construction of subjectivity.
The relationship between identity and identification is a
complex one that in the case of melancholia my reading of
Freud suggests amounts to a self-reflexive fusion of the two.

Melancholia is essentially the product of a grievance with the
loved object, which although it has disappointed or indeed
deserted the subject cannot be given up and mourned as lost,
but is internalized by the process of identification. That is, that
which cannot be grieved – mourned – becomes a grievance, and
persists in psychic life. Freud discovered in his treatment of
hysterics that the recovery in language of the originary
experience which precipitated the hysteria and the associated
but split-off affect relieves the symptom, and disengages the
sufferer from the compulsion to repeat the hysterical phenom-
ena. The melancholic memorialization I am proposing embodies
the search for an identity through language. 'Much of the
distress', and our pleasure, in Forrest-Thomson's poems as Raitt
observes 'comes from her feeling that identity and desire occur
somewhere in language, but continually escape its structurings'
(Raitt, 305). Something always escapes along the chain of
language, chain of associations, and it is that 'unspeakable'
which poetry attempts to capture in its net of words and spaces,
which analysis attempts to recover for therapeutic effect. The
irony being, as Forrest-Thomson knew, that as soon as the
particular, especially if 'another human being', by implication a
lover, is captured (or the repressed memory recalled to
consciousness), 'being caught as a poetic fiction, as a real
person he is gone' (CP 264). This is the theme of 'Sonnet', where
'the other person is the personification of the other, the
unknown, the external world', the lost object of the restless
metonymies of desire.

The poem is balanced on a delicate irony, aided by reversals of expectation – expectation set up both by the form of the poem, and by the use of language within it. In 'Never so separate trying to be two', the ending of the line, always a significant position in poetry, is the opposite of the expected 'one'. Of course, for the narcissistic melancholic it is precisely 'being two' – self and other – that is so impossible. Echoes of other poems, most evidently Donne's 'Busie olde foole, unruly Sunne',[35] are from that literary unconscious of the text which we subsume under the heading of intertextuality: other discourses, all that past, half-remembered material of Western culture that Angela Carter called the 'folklore of the intelligentsia',[36] which provided for Forrest-Thomson such a rich source of allusion, imitation, parody and pastiche.

The transference which in the analytic situation, the 'talking cure' (Freud, III, 30), occurs between patient and analyst, in writing takes place between poet and poem and then again between poem and reader. The therapeutics of language always require an intermediary. 'Sonnet' is a development of themes that appear in other poems, most notably 'Gemini' and 'Canzon', both of which also recall Lacan's Mirror Stage and the impossibility of seeking the truth of the self in the other. In 'Sonnet' the imaginative possibilities inherent in this situation have undergone further development. The speaking subject of 'Sonnet' has accepted, however ironically, separateness; no longer yearns for an impossible blissful merging, but also understands the power of bonds between two subjects, alienated in language, their means of communication and creation of their world: 'Words were made to prevent us near'.

This subtle line concludes an ironic, painful address to 'the other' (in both senses), and the dislocated syntax preserves the sense of 'us near' as 'us close', while the use of 'prevent' (in the sense of impede) disrupts the reader's conventional expectation – a form of naturalization – of 'bring' or 'keep'. Words literally come between us: they simultaneously unite and separate, like the hyphen. They also come before us, since we are born into language, and Forrest-Thomson's line preserves the seventeenth-century use of 'prevent' as 'to come before'.[37] Words come before our existence as subjects, alienated in language, and are at once our means of communication and creation of our

91

world. They mark our capacity for union and for separation; embody communication and the blocks to understanding: we are divided by a common language. Negotiating this problem of articulation as the word is used in 'Sagittarius', in both senses of utterance and jointing, connecting different elements, gave Forrest-Thomson the major theme of her work. In her poems she increasingly found (as I will discuss further in relation to 'Cordelia') a way to express the apparently inarticulable, through her use of structures of parodic juxtaposition: 'in poetry as in psychoanalysis, language is pushed to its limits, and becomes a struggle with the inexpressible'.[38]

Immediately after discussing 'Sonnet' in the preface to *On the Periphery*, Forrest-Thomson speaks of the 'three quests' of her writing in that collection. The first is for a style suitable to her subject, the second for another subject than that typically modernist theme of 'the difficulty of writing', and the third another traditional thematic of lyric, as she notes:

> the quest for another human being. Indeed such equation of love with knowledge and the idea of style as their reconciliation is as old as the art itself, for the other person is the personification of the other, the unknown, the external world and all one's craft is necessary to catch him. And, of course, being caught as a poetic fiction, as a real person he is gone. (*CP* 264)

'If I write a song for you', using all 'my craft', 'To that extent you are gone': once the experience is realized in words, expressed, discharged, it is finished as an act of rememory and transformed into a memorial for something that is past. 'We are all always alone': in this poem the thematic synthesis is given at the end of the first verse, and worked through the image complexes of the rest of the poem. These incorporate Donne's lovers, the erotics of trying to 'finger myself from you', and the pathos of saying 'I love you' while denying it, since that avoids self-exposure, though one wonders what 'irony knows what we'll say' might be. Perhaps that the employment of irony, always closely associated with parody, inevitably involves a proprioception of the response of the other. As Hutcheon remarks in *Irony's Edge*, 'an attribution of irony could act to attenuate the effect...perhaps even of a boast or a declaration of love: for the ironist, irony means never having to say you're sorry'.[39]

With that self-reflexiveness characteristic of Forrest-Thom-

92

son's poetry, attempts 'to free myself by my craft' from this trap of melancholia – of which this poem must clearly be an instance – have the 'I' of the poem twisting and turning in an attempt to avoid the realization of the first verse, of the distanciation of language, the indissoluble separateness of subjectivity in the world of representations. Thereby Forrest-Thomson finds a way of saying what she needs to in spite of saying it is impossible, and by the same techniques that govern the verse forms (form and content operating in each other's field as well as their own); by an ironic withholding that forecloses the possibility of rejection and is a pun on the performativity of poetry: 'accept the wish for the deed'; accept the fantasy for the actuality, imaginary fulfilment for the impossible real.

She recognizes in *Poetic Artifice* 'how hard it is to tread the line between the imagination and the unimagined "real", how difficult it is – since language is common to both "reality" and "imagination" – to attain the artifice of eternity through language' (*PA* 17). And as Freud discovered, the register of the unconscious is a timeless zone, where no reality testing is possible, and where one's own immortality goes omnipotently unquestioned. The phrase 'the artifice of eternity', itself borrowed from Yeats's elegiac 'Sailing to Byzantium' which also plays with these themes of the transience of 'Whatever is begotten, born, and dies'[40] contrasted with the timelessness and immortality of art, here indicates a similar timelessness. Poets know that artifice suspends time and decay, utters a valediction of mourning in favour of a memorialization: a melancholia. It is an attempt to prevent or circumvent the experience of loss which is the emotional theme of the poem, that loss which is also the affective charge released from the poem: 'We are all always alone'. The melancholic theme of memorialization by artifice in denial of personal loss is one which Forrest-Thomson took from her predecessor, the greatest sonnet writer, whose lines in Sonnet 18 hover over hers:

> But thy eternal summer shall not fade
> Nor lose possession of that fair thou owest;
> Nor shall Death brag thou wander'st in his shade,
> When in eternal lines to time thou growest:
> So long as men can breathe, or eyes can see,
> So long lives this, and this gives life to thee.

93

'The shadow of the object fell upon the ego' is Freud's memorable and poignant, even melancholic description of the outcome of the melancholic refusal to relinquish the inevitably lost object (Freud, XIV, 249). In the preface to *On the Periphery*, immediately prior to introducing 'Sonnet', Forrest-Thomson refers to 'The Lady of Shalott' as 'both the end of this quest for a lost imaginative freedom...and a beginning which, freed from sterile self-absorption, will move on to create new artifices of eternity' (*CP* 264). These are, I suggest, just such refined and haunting melancholias of parodic technique that we see in operation in 'Sonnet'. The irony being, the paradox which would have delighted Mann's Devil, that self-absorption – though here far from sterile – is precisely the outcome of a melancholic structure; one which seeks to preserve the past of poetic form and language, through artifice, within the body of the poetry of the present.

In *Artifice of Absorption* Charles Bernstein asserts that 'Loss is as much a part of the semantic process as/ discharge is a part of the biological process' (Bernstein, 12). This perceptive couplet implies a similar view of the relationship between language and psychic functioning. Poetic language, in particular the structures and devices of artifice, are then part of the poetic equivalent of the psychic devices of repression, identification and embodiment which seek to restrain that loss, contain that discharge, or at least temporarily suspend it, as required by Forrest-Thomson's preferred system of naturalization.

She calls 'Sonnet' 'the love poem I have tried throughout to write straight' (*CP* 264), and in his 1976 review Porter prefers, rather than to explore her connections with contemporary theory or the Cambridge poetry scene, 'to consider her work as the approach of a brilliantly analytical mind to the problem of the expression of emotion in a much worked-over art (poetry)'. Her solution to this problem, I believe, is found in her capacity to create a situation in language through the juxtaposition of different elements of discourse (an essentially parodic technique), in which working through the different levels of language in the poem will culminate in reuniting the thematic synthesis and the affective charge split off by the poem's structure. This creates the correlative for the reader to the process discussed in her thesis of the 'thinking-through' that needs to go on in writing a poem, so that 'poetry provides us with the *experience* of thinking, rather than with the thought itself' (PK 125). In 'Sonnet', as in 'Ducks & Rabbits', her poetry can provide us with just that experience of thinking physically which we call emotion.

The emotion most typical of Forrest-Thomson's work of this period is, as Porter suggests, unhappiness. But where Porter sees also 'the mental toughness necessary to record it and outface it', I find the more unusual ability to turn ordinary unhappiness into an art of language which can help us think through, intellectually and physically, experiences of loss and distress. As Wittgenstein says, with his usual combination of the perceptive and the prosaic:

> a poet's words can pierce us. And that is of course *causally* connected with the use that they have in our life. And it is also connected with the way in which, conformably to this use, we let our thoughts roam up and down in the familiar surroundings of the words. (Wittgenstein2, 27:155)

Living with poems written on the periphery of what it is possible to do with our words can create the possibility of experiencing a different form of life, a motive which activates the work of Language writers in their explorations of subjectivity and experience.

Coda: *Cordelia*

I wish I could tenderly lift from the dark side of history, voices
that are anonymous, slighted – inarticulate.

(Susan Howe, 'There Are Not Leaves Enough to Crown to Cover to Crown
to Cover', from *The Europe of Trusts*)

LEAR: ... what can you say to draw
A third more opulent than your sisters? Speak.
CORDELIA: Nothing, my lord.
LEAR: Nothing?
CORDELIA: Nothing.
LEAR: Nothing will come of nothing: speak again.
...
LEAR: So young and so untender?
CORDELIA: So young, my lord, and true.

(William Shakespeare, *King Lear*, Act 1, scene 1)

While Forrest-Thomson uses parody throughout her later poems
as part of her 'kit for transforming the non-poetic into the
poem' (*PA* 129), rather than to achieve a satiric or burlesque
effect, it is particularly in her recuperations of aspects of
Romantic and Victorian poetry in the poems of *On the Periphery*
where the connection between parody and gender is made. A
form of parody developed from her use of other language-
games in that of poetry becomes the most important technique
in the long poem 'Cordelia or "A poem should not mean, but
be"', but there are other poems in the collection which prepare
the ground for the negotiations with parody and gender that
appear in 'Cordelia'.

Forrest-Thomson's uneasy poetic relationship with gender –
an issue closely related to the question of the construction of
identity in language – is influenced by her engagement with
Eliot's idea of 'poetic impersonality' in 'Tradition and the

96

Individual Talent', and in particular his separation of 'the man who suffers and the mind which creates' (Eliot2, 41). This distinction is a precursor to that now customarily made between the poet and the 'I' set up by the poem, and a rejection of the biographical fallacy which collapses the two. In *Poetic Artifice* there are two citations of Eliot's phrase in connection with Sylvia Plath (*PA* 113, 159). The interpretation of Plath's work often still suffers from that fallacy, and Forrest-Thomson's second allusion forms part of a critique of Ted Hughes's 'inappropriate idea of a poet's relation to his poems', that is precisely his collapsing of the distinction between the poet and the speaking subject of the poem. Forrest-Thomson attempts, if briefly, to remedy the neglect of 'Plath's poems as exponents of Artifice', and it is indeed interesting to reflect on the linguistic and formal innovation which characterizes Plath's later poems, and their connections with the techniques of Language writing.

In *Poetic Artifice* the feminine pronouns 'she' and 'her' are used throughout with reference to the work of Plath but when it comes to references to Forrest-Thomson's own poems, 'Pastoral' and 'The Lady of Shalott', the case is different. She refers to herself as 'the poet', and while ironically acknowledging her equivocation by an immediate parenthesis: '(having had the effrontery to use my own poems as examples I now hide behind my role)' (*PA* 124), she then proceeds to refer to this figure – that is herself – as 'he'. At the time of writing, this could possibly have seemed like a gesture towards the 'process of depersonalization' Eliot proposed (Eliot2, 40), perhaps in this instance to distance the figure of the poet from that of the critic writing theory, doubly aware of not only the 'poet's relation to his poems' but also the relation of the critic to those poems: a characteristic *dédoublement*. But it is a curious and awkward manoeuvre nonetheless, pregnant with irony; an uneasy disavowal of gender which finds another explanation in Forrest-Thomson's earlier discussion of the position of 'the twentieth-century poet' who is also invariably gendered masculine. 'I say "he"', she writes, 'because he is a mythical figure, a familiar compound ghost, metaphysicist-metaphysician, tribal outcast' (*PA* 86). But he is also specifically 'Thomas Stearns Eliot', with whose technical abilities she strongly identified. And in introducing the concept of artistic impersonality Eliot yokes 'the process of depersonalization and its relation to the sense of tradition'. By choosing to employ the masculine 'he' to characterize the poet who is herself, Forrest-Thomson seeks to establish herself by gender and contiguity as part of the dual lineages of poetic tradition and of poetic innovation, in direct descent from Donne and Eliot. In 'Cordelia' we see the development of a more sophisticated negotiation of poetic gender as part of a complex articulation of poetic identity in that poem.

Gender begins to be refigured in Forrest-Thomson's work of this period by her employment of a Persephone figure in 'The Lady of Shalott', and of course in 'The Garden of Proserpine'. Both take their titles from well-known poems by famous nineteenth-century male poets, and male poets have traditionally apostrophized female figures, and exploited them as both structural and thematic devices. They have used female fictional personae to hold their poems together, either entirely within the poem as its subject like Tennyson's 'Lady of Shalott', or as the addressees or objects of poems, like so many of Donne's and Empson's clearly female 'you's. The fictional females, who of course are also related to the concept of the female 'Muse' beloved of male poets, are frequently dangerous and/or occult – certainly to the male subjects of the poems in which they appear. These mutating figures, fictional females, are under the control of male poets for whom they are instruments of artifice. They are 'denizens of Pastoral' (*PA* 118) in the sense that they are creations of artifice and function on the structural as well as thematic levels of the poem, like Swinburne's 'ferocious Faustine', of whom Forrest-Thomson says:

> She exists, then, not simply as a necessary fiction but as subject to that goddess who rules the realm of Artifice. She is Persephone, queen of the dead and bringer of life, both one and three. ... Only when considered as an organising principle in the verse is her true complexity perceived. (*PA* 118)

Tennyson's 'The Lady of Shalott', who is also designated 'a creature of pastoral... an organising formal principle' (*PA* 123), and Forrest-Thomson's ambivalent recuperation of her, form part of a lineage of these female necessary fictions and organizing principles, whose very names and locations can be

98

mere conveniences for the sake of rhyme and metre, like Shalott
and Camelot. They can exist in both the verbal and 'non-verbal'
or formal worlds, and bridge the two. To some extent Forrest-
Thomson uses them to the same end, but she also subverts the
masculine dominance of their construction in the background
poem by foregrounding their constructedness, and the instru-
mentality with which they are regarded by the male poets. Thus
she returns to them some degree of 'autonomy', releasing them
from their source function as objects to the male poet's subject;
this is the first stage in what develops in 'Cordelia' into a
feminine negotiation of the Oedipal situation of 'the tradition'.

Forrest-Thomson's recuperations of such female figures pro-
pose a complex and sophisticated female Oedipal strategy. In
these poems we see the beginning of a powerful project to
redirect the flow of that stream of canonical poetry which is
predominantly male, and reinscribe its gender. This can be read
as a double early Oedipal gesture, simultaneously repudiating
and identifying with – through incorporation – the primary
figure. In the early Oedipal configuration, this figure is the
mother. In this literary instance, it is not the mother in relation to
whom the female 'child' has to make this move, but rather the
literary historical 'fathers', who in this case constitute the primary
figure. Of course for a woman poet, as for the female child, this
Oedipal negotiation will inevitably be more complex than for the
male, especially since the Freudian model itself, and that model
as taken up by Harold Bloom, infers two masculine generations.[1]

The self-consciousness of the Oedipality of Forrest-Thomson's
poetic piracies, plagiarisms and acknowledged citations in the
parodic structure of 'Cordelia' (where the name of Oedipus is
conspicuous by his absence) is supported by the humorous
injunction to read the classical legends in their source texts, not
in Freud:

> Read it in the *Iliad*, read it in the *Odyssey*,
> Do not read it in Freud who is always wrong
> Although even Freud didn't deserve a son like Lacan.

> (*CP* 108)

Forrest-Thomson took much of her emphasis on the im-
portance of linking what she calls 'the past of poetic form and a
vision of imaginative possibilities in the future' (C. 1), from her

reading of Eliot's influential 'Tradition and the Individual Talent'. This essay also provided the provisional or working title in her notebook entitled *Pomes* to the poem which became 'Cordelia or "A poem should not mean but be"', her attempt at the epic, traditionally the hallmark of poetic stature. The question of 'influence' or poetic relations is a complex one, and again involves a double Oedipal negotiation, here transposed to Eliot's theory. His argument regarding the relationship between innovation and tradition provided a template for her own parodic negotiation of continuity and discontinuity in language, especially in the conspicuous intertextuality of her works' relation to the work of previous poets. Eliot particularly remarks on the paradoxical nature of individual poetic innovation, that it is inevitably founded upon previous example:

> We dwell with satisfaction upon the poet's difference from his predecessors, especially his immediate predecessors... we shall often find that not only the best, but the most individual parts of his work may be those in which the dead poets, his ancestors, assert their immortality most vigorously...
>
> No poet, no artist of any art, has his complete meaning alone. His significance, his appreciation is the appreciation of his relation to the dead poets and artists. You cannot value him alone; you must set him, for contrast and comparison, among the dead. (Eliot2, 38)

Some of Forrest-Thomson's incorporations of other poets' work, such as the Coda taken from Arnaut Daniel in 'Canzon', stand breathtakingly alone, in virtually their original form, and yet subtly shifted and intensified by their relocation, their, in Hutcheon's term, 'trans-contextualization' (Hutcheon, 8). It is worth recalling here Forrest-Thomson's emphatic appropriation from Wittgenstein in her poems 'The Hyphen' and 'The Blue Book', that it is the context in which we occur that teaches us our meaning. Lexical units that are thus relocated carry with them the atmosphere and resonance of their source, but their meaning is given either an ironic twist or a powerful intensification: in the case of Forrest-Thomson's poems frequently both. As with her reading of Eliot's literary criticism into her own work, it is unwise either to take a statement entirely at face value, or to be entirely certain that her interrogation by incorporation is necessarily ironic.

Forrest-Thomson takes Eliot's second injunction, 'You cannot
value [the poet] alone; you must set him, for contrast and
comparison, among the dead', literally as well as figuratively in
'Cordelia'. As well as quoting from and alluding to the history of
poetry and poetic artifice from classical times (Homer,
Sophocles, Euripides), through Renaissance practice as exem-
plified by Shakespeare, to the contemporary through the figure
of Prynne, and of course herself, she also sets in the poem
listings of classical, Renaissance and Modern dead, beginning
with Dante's Beatrice and the Medici family. And Dante was
one of Eliot's primary influences:

> The word you want is Dante.
> He said he loved Beatrice. Whatever he did
> He didn't love Beatrice. At least the
> Beatrice Portinari whom history gives.
> He knew her and the point about all these
> Florentines is that they all were
> Killing each other or dying of rapid
> Consumption. Beatrice died; Rossetti painted her
> Cutting Dante in the street. Botticelli
> Painted the rest: Simonetta Vespucci
> Died of a rapid consumption (age 23)
> Guliano dei Medici murdered by the altar rail (age 19)
> Guido Cavalcanti died in exile (age 35)
> Dante dei Aligeri died in exile (age 90)
> Lorenzo dei Medici who lives for ever
> Since he stayed there and commissioned
> The paintings, and poems and statues
> And if he also commissioned the deaths
> I don't blame him.
>
> (*CP* 104–5)

Forrest-Thomson draws attention here again through this
breathless catalogue to the fact that persons, even historical
persons or the living, once set in a poem are not 'themselves' but
fictional contructions: Dante's Beatrice is not 'the/ Beatrice
Portinari whom history gives'. This passage also, and with
humour more than melancholy – a humour that rings in her
voice in the splendid reading she gave of 'Cordelia' at the 1975
Cambridge Poetry Festival – invokes the traditional theme of
'Sonnet', of immortality through art, through artifice.[2]
Of course, the issue of response to previous example is as

likely to occasion the rejection of earlier practice as its adoption, but in neither case can the process of reinscription be avoided. Forrest-Thomson's own capacity for alternation between resistance to tradition – an innovative disruption of expectation – and the adoption of formal techniques of rhyme and metre inherited from that tradition as well as its themes and thematic personae, is particularly productive of powerful poetry. She finds the middle area, on the periphery of both tradition and innovation, through an articulation of parody.

In 'Cordelia' the beginning of a move towards establishing the inheritance of the female line set up by her use of Persephone is developed in her reworkings of patriarchal myth:

> I, Helen, I Iseult, I Guenevere,
> I Clytemnestra and many more to come.
> I did it, I myself, killing the King my father
> Killing the King my mother, joining the King my brother.

(CP 108)

A description of descent, of identification, which does not ignore the lethal implications of the process of inheritance, succession, and the Oedipal situation. Her assertion and identification of the poetic 'I' here is restricted neither to powerful mythical figures of women, nor to a subordinate position, whatever the inheritance from the predominantly male tradition; a tradition which is exemplified by the allusion in her lines to 'The Waste Land', which is itself recalling *The Tempest*:

> Musing upon the king my brother's wreck
> And on the king my father's death before him.

(Eliot1, 70)

Of course in *The Tempest* it is the male Ferdinand who is 'Weeping again the King my father's wrack',[3] following Prospero's relation to his daughter Miranda of the story of Ferdinand's father and his brother's usurpation of Prospero's dukedom. These shifts of gender and their Oedipal implications are an important part of the theme of succession, usurpation, violence and violent death, betrayal and love in 'Cordelia', which twines familial and romantic relations and murderousness.

By mingling her accounts of, or references to, events in history and events in art, Forrest-Thomson interrogates the dichotomy between art and event, which Eliot had insisted 'is always absolute' (Eliot2, 42). From the perspective of art itself, of poetry, that difference is elided: both become fictionalized when taken into, incorporated in a construction of artifice. The figures and stories which dash across the stage of this poem range from those of Agammemnon (*sic*) and Clytemnestra, the Medici and Romeo and Juliet, Richards I, II and III, the Joyces, the Shelleys, and the contemporary 'J.H. Prynne, the memorable poet' (*CP* 106) and 'Veronica Forrest-Thomson' (*CP* 107), who equally become thematic and structural figures, figures of speech rather than figures of flesh. And her articulation of the proper relation between interpretation and suspended naturalization is Forrest-Thomson's suggested solution to the aesthetic problem of the attempt to transform experience into art.

Towards the conclusion of 'Cordelia', Forrest-Thomson goes on to assert the status of the 'I' of this poem, who is clearly a poet though not necessarily to be identified with the poet who is writing, even if her name is given as part of the substance of the poem:

> I am not Prince Thomas Aquinas F.H. Eliot[4]
> I am not an attendant lord either.
> I am the king who lives.

> (*CP* 109)

Again this incorporates a quotation from Eliot ('F.H.' being Bradley, who like Aquinas is materially 'incorporated' here by 'Eliot'), for the allusion is to 'The Love Song of J. Alfred Prufrock' (1917), and one of Eliot's masculine – if emasculated – poetic personae:

> No! I am not Prince Hamlet, nor was meant to be;
> Am an attendant lord, one that will do
> To swell a progress, start a scene or two,
> Advise the prince...
> ...
> Almost, at times, the Fool.

> (Eliot1, 17)

And of course, the Fool appears in *King Lear*, whose daughter Cordelia's name entitles Forrest-Thomson's poem but who, like Oedipus, never actually appears in the body of the poem. Perhaps inevitably, since Cordelia was remarkable for silence: love and silence, a figure to whom Susan Howe (a poet associated with Language) also gives voice in 'WHITE FOOLSCAP/Book of Cordelia', and 'God's Spies' in *The Liberties*.[5] The very use of Cordelia's name evokes that silencing of the female poetic voice occasioned by the significant exclusion of woman poets from the literary canon, and in particular from the discourse of the epic.

Forrest-Thomson's own poetic statement of identity – 'I' am King not Fool – refutes the self-deprecation of 'Prufrock''s modest claims to identity. It also underlines the importance of the fact, stressed by Forrest-Thomson, that the 'I' set up by the poem is a construct rather than an individual personality – so often naturalized as the poet. This is also established by Eliot:

> the poet has, not a 'personality' to express, but a particular medium, which is only a medium and not a personality, in which impressions and experiences combine in peculiar and unexpected ways. (Eliot2, 42)

This poetic rather than personal identity has a flexibility which is created within the medium of poetry itself: the capacity to take a plurality of positions, usually available to human subjects only in dreams, including shifts of gender and the assuming of historical and literary roles and functions. The epic medium of 'Cordelia' can combine impressions and experiences in ways impossible outside the licence of poetic language, juxtaposing feminine and masculine identities and personae from different periods of literature and history with the here and now, historical identities and locations of the poet and her associates, like Prynne. She particularly draws on the classical period, since the epic is not only a classic form but produced the most important examples of the male-dominated genre: 'Read it in the *Iliad*, read it in the *Odyssey*' (CP 108). This combination of here and now with there and then in 'Cordelia' offers a commentary on the transferential aspect of poetic composition: how it oscillates between the past and the present in both form and theme. Elements are taken from the past and transferred onto the present, since the main traditional themes of poetry, of love and of mortality, and of the triumph of artifice over time, are themselves 'eternal' concerns.

In addition to affirming the continuity of poetic identity, through the medium of poetry – in this case of parodic epic, at once serious and humorous – Forrest-Thomson also interrogates identity (which might be either false or assumed) before discussing her own, under the guise of answering an implied question from an implied interlocutor:

> I may look stupid but I'm not
> So simple as to think your name
> Is Elizabeth Brown. Well. All right
> My name is Veronica Forrest-Thomson.

(CP 106–7)

And thereby turns herself into a poetic persona or 'I', simultaneously factual and fictional. As she remarks in *Poetic Artifice*: 'Of course I have been maintaining all along that the personages and decor in poems are convenient fictions, and that so are the poet and reader' (*PA* 69).

Typically, from the stage of writing in the *Pomes* notebook to the final published version there is an increase of ironic distance, signalled by a characteristic bathetic undercutting of the grandiosity of the assertions of identity in the earlier version. The following list of identifications is from *Pomes* (I have preserved the manuscript lineation):

> I, Helen, I, Iseult, I, Sappho who was queen
>   of the lesbians and like all good queens lives
> I, Clytemnestra, I Guinevere, and many more
>   who are still to come
> I am I Veronica, truth-seeking, truth-
>   finder, bringer of victory

It is worth noting that Sappho is omitted from the list of identifications in the published version, and that in the preparatory stage it is Sappho, as a 'good queen' – in imitation of the humorous classification in *1066 and All That*[6] of kings as either Good or Bad – who 'lives'. In 'Cordelia' this becomes 'the king who lives', albeit a king of questionable gender: that is, the king as function rather than person, just as the poem sets up an 'I' as a function, rather than a personality. Again humorously – and this is often a very funny poem – in 'Cordelia' we find the insertion of 'muck-raking' among the more traditional epic formulaic attributes in the published version of her adaptation of the classic lines:

I, Veronica did it, truth-finding, truth-seeking
Muck-raking, bringing victory.

(CP 108–9)

But it is to love and its pains; and death; and repetition and
poetry to which she returns at the conclusion of the poem:

I am the king who lives.
Spring surprised us, running through the market square
And we stopped in Prynne's rooms in a shower of pain
And went on in sunlight into the University Library
And ate yogurt and talked for an hour.
You, You, grab the reins.
Drink as much as you can and love as much as you can
And work as much as you can
For you can't do anything when you are dead.

The motto of this poem heed
And do you it employ:
Waste not and want not while you're here
The possibles of joy.

(CP 109)

Her reference here to the opening of 'The Waste Land' is a
parodic homage to Eliot's work, embedded in the traditional
theme of the transience of life – and love. This, a postmodern
use of parody, can choose between and even alternate between
humorous irony and serious tribute, as it negotiates the double
part of conservation and transgression, tradition and resistance.
Forrest-Thomson preserves the power and atmosphere of Eliot's
most celebrated poem as he preserved that of Chaucer's
'Prologue' to The Canterbury Tales, in tribute to the history of
poetry in English these poets and poems span. She puts a spin
on the affective level of the poem in parody of Eliot's conversion
of Chaucer's 'Aprille with his shoures soote'[7] into 'April is the
cruellest month', but she moves further into the body of Eliot's
poem, into his first intercut narrative, while relocating it in time
by changing the season and in place by moving to Cambridge.
Eliot's poem reads:

Summer surprised us, coming up over the Starnbergersee
With a shower of rain; we stopped in the colonnade,
And went on in sunlight, into the Hofgarten,
And drank coffee, and talked for an hour.

(Eliot1, 63)

106

Forrest-Thomson's unique contribution – the transgression, the innovation, the resistance – is supplied by the sharpening of the intellectual emotion of Eliot's poem: an emotion evoked by the piling up of the images into a visceral tug of grief. This is achieved by the minute shift of one letter, from 'rain' to 'pain' in which the accompanying shift from realist description to surreal immediacy makes emotional sense and takes the intellectual breath away. It is all the more poignant for its embedding in prosaic description, and carries the double charge of Eliot's construction and Forrest-Thomson's reconstruction. In *Pomes* an earlier and considerably flatter version took more from Eliot, including the persona of 'Marie', humorously reworked for identification with the Scottish 'Veronica Forrest-Thomson' already included in the poem:

> Spring surprised us coming through the market and stopped in
> Prynne's rooms
> And went on in sunlight into the University Library
> And drank coffee and talked for an hour
> I am certainly not a Russian, I come from Scotland
> terribly English
> Marie, Marie, grab the reins
> Don't fall off and drink as much as you can
> For you can't drink/,work/ love when you're dead.

The transformation of this into an impassioned invocation of the addressee of the poem, 'you' – implicitly at one level always the reader – is a remarkable example of Forrest-Thomson's dexterity with Artifice, her capacity to change gear in mid-flight by the employment of what she called the non-meaningful aspects of language, here primarily of rhythm and metre.

Forrest-Thomson's own attempt to circumvent the problem of the privileged relation of the poem to experience through her concept of suspended naturalization puts the focus on mediation in poetic language rather than immediacy of assimilation, or paraphrase. In her own poetry this resulted in the use of techniques which can hold off the emotion of the poem until the final working through of the thematic synthesis at its conclusion. By comparing the endings of the versions we have of 'Cordelia' we can see the subtleties of artifice involved in creating this kind of tension and resolution. It is a risky business subverting expectation to this degree, risking a collapse into bathos, a collapse held at bay by a flair for timing, and by the use of a postmodern parody that does not of necessity involve either denigration or amusement. The use of past poetry, of Eliot here, stabilizes and confers depth and dignity on the closing lines, containing the energy of the poem to allow the poet to move into direct address, and a ballad-style statement of the poem's theme, uniting the discursive, conceptual aspect of experience with the empirical immediacy of experience. This synthesis is what Forrest-Thomson understood Eliot to have achieved in his poetry, and which he attempted to theorize through his concept of the objective correlative. This is her discussion of it in *Poetic Artifice*:

> The famous fusion of thought and experience to which Eliot alerted the century, the interaction of discursive and empirical imagery, seemed to provide a way of articulating immediate experience while engaging in the process of mediation. The result was the conviction that innovation in technique, which detaches the poet from his reader's idea of poetry and its relation to experience, could be made to retain its hold on the accepted world of discourse if one asserted a connection with past poetry. (*PA* 81)

It is the life of the emotion *within* the poem that is of concern to Forrest-Thomson, as it was to Eliot. She took his technique one stage further in the disappearance of the emotion from the surface of the poem and its final release at the end. What is perceived is not Forrest-Thomson's emotion, but the emotion of the poem itself, as translated by the reader. The 'connection with past poetry' anchors the reader in 'the accepted world of discourse'; keeps them from getting lost in discontinuity, in innovative technique, or resorting to premature external naturalization. Her earlier practices of embedded quotation and allusion develop in 'Cordelia' into a sustained and sophisticated use of parodic technique to maintain connections simultaneously between different discourses, different languages, different aspects of the history of poetry and poetic language, and to disrupt expectation, effect discontinuity and transgress the authority on which they initially draw. Forrest-Thomson evolved this technique in her search for the middle ground in which new meanings, new 'imaginative possibilities in the future' as she says in the preface to *Cordelia*, can develop; a middle ground on the periphery of both tradition and innovation where what was previously silenced can begin to speak.

In connection with which, a final word on titles and subtitles, statement and subversion. The change from the working title 'Tradition and the Individual Talent' to 'Cordelia or "A poem should not mean but be"' reflects a major shift of emphasis from pastoral to parody. Not only does the figure of Cordelia herself betoken female, daughterly silence and sacrifice to a demanding and deluded patriarch, but the ironic subtitle reinforces the theme of silencing, and its refusal, for the elegant syntactic parellelism of Archibald MacLeish's 'Ars Poetica' from which it is taken begins:

> A poem should be palpable and mute
> As a globed fruit,
>
> Dumb
> As old medallions to the thumb,
>
> Silent as the sleeve-worn stone
> Of casement ledges where the moss has grown –
>
> A poem should be wordless
> As the flight of birds.[8]

If a poem is as wordless as Shakespeare's Cordelia, then perhaps it can only share the same fate. Yet MacLeish's poem concludes with the haunting minimalism of:

> For all the history of grief
> An empty doorway and a maple leaf.
>
> For love
> The leaning grasses and two lights above the sea –
>
> A poem should not mean
> But be.

This employs a technique that contains the rudiments of the postmodern parody I suggest Forrest-Thomson employs in 'Cordelia'. Parallelism that is not simply repetition, like parody, invariably 'implies both similarity and difference'.[9] The main distinction between the two lies in parody's inherently transgressive function, which always shadows its preservation of similarity; difference is not of itself necessarily transgressive. Forrest-Thomson's use of MacLeish's concluding line as subtitle

109

is a paradigmatic instance of her approach to and use of parody as technique: 'stressing connection on the thematic level by taking another language as its theme' (*PA* 113). The emphasis falls on *stressing* the connection, not just making it, or even enabling it to be made by the reader. For Forrest-Thomson the connection, the continuity, is vital to intelligibility, and it is the conventional structural ground that permits intelligible innovation in technique, and hence a vision of future imaginative possibilities. Just what that vision might be, has indeed become in the work of other poets, is my next concern.

5

language, Language,
L=A=N=G=U=A=G=E

One poet, poet and critic, who if she had lived would have
found them sympathetic was Veronica Forrest-Thomson... her
own poetry, and her critical book *Poetic Artifice*, were moving
very much towards the 'language' poetry position.

(Edwin Morgan, *Language, Poetry, and Language Poetry*)

It is one of literary history's ironies that language writing, a
movement challenging the social and rhetorical prerogatives of
capital, has become a semiproper name that itself bestows a
certain amount of cultural capital upon those it covers.

(Bob Perelman, *The Marginalization of Poetry*)

By recognising itself as the *philosophy of practice in language*,
poetry can work to search out the preconditions of a liberated
language within the existing social fact.

(Ron Silliman, 'Disappearance of the Word, Appearance of the World')

The university is the 500 pound gorilla at the party of poets.

(Ron Silliman, 'Canons and Institutions: New Hope for the Disappeared',
from *The Politics of Poetic Form*)

The most striking engagement with the issues that concerned
Forrest-Thomson – particularly in *Poetic Artifice* – appears in
Charles Bernstein's long poem of poetics, his 'Essay on
Criticism', *Artifice of Absorption*. In this remarkable work, first
published in 1987 as a special issue of the magazine *Paper Air*
and later included in *A Poetics*, Bernstein deals with many of the
major debates which inform Forrest-Thomson's work: questions
of the relationship between subjectivity and language, poetry as
a vehicle for experience, poetry as knowledge, and the position
of the reader in relation to the text. In Bernstein's text these are

absorbed into and filtered through an engagement with Forrest-Thomson's dominant concerns with poetic artifice and naturalization. Her two key concepts find their correlatives in *Artifice of Absorption*'s two sections: 'Meaning and Artifice', and 'Absorption and Impermeability'.

We have already seen how artifice calls attention self-reflexively to its own operations and to the way in which language constructs the world. And how readers choose, particularly in the case of poetry, to engage with language which is distinctly different from the ordinary language of communication, and then seem driven to reduce its difference to an assimilable narrative. Bernstein writes of Forrest-Thomson that:

> her terminology is intended to foreground artifice
> as much as possible & for this reason she wishes
> to cede as little as possible to the conventional
> semantic arena – a decision that makes her book, if
> flawed in this respect, so powerfully informative
> in the first place.

(Bernstein, 9)

Although Forrest-Thomson did not so much reject meaning as attempt to resist the reader's tendency to premature reference to the world outside the text, Bernstein is right to suggest that she wants – a desire he clearly shares – to 'cede as little as possible to the *conventional* semantic arena', to permit a textual polysemy which makes 'many Naturalisations possible and none certain' (*PA* 80). Bernstein persuasively problematizes the designation of any aspect of language as 'non-meaningful' or 'non-semantic' because of the danger that this would 'restrict meaning to/ the exclusively recuperable elements of language' (Bernstein, 8), a limitation which would exclude the unconscious or partially recoverable aspects of language that are vital to poetry. As he indicates, meaning is only possible 'in a context of conscious & nonconscious,/ recuperable & unrecoverable, dynamics'. This implicitly subscribes to Wittgenstein's view that the context in which the words occur indicates the meaning, with the reading of 'context' extended to include the unconscious and unrecoverable, the *pulsions* of language.

While recuperability is significant for, if not coextensive with, meaning, the identification of the 'conscious' with the

112

'recuperable', and the 'nonconscious' with the 'unrecoverable' set up here by Bernstein's syntactic parallelism may be an oversimplification. What he calls the 'nonconscious' of a poem can, in significant part, be recuperated through a reading which takes in all the levels of poetic language, as recommended in *Poetic Artifice*. Forrest-Thomson's move, which Bernstein takes a stage further by refusing to designate any aspect of language as non-meaningful, seeks to shift the emphasis in reading – and indeed writing – poetry from the *primacy* of meaning, to refute the view of meaning as an extractable 'essence' of the poem: for as Bernstein observes 'the poem said in any/ other way is not the poem' (Bernstein, 11). Forrest-Thomson's rearrangement of the weighting of the contribution of form and content to the poem in traditional poetry is taken up and progressed in the work of the Language writers, who increasingly destabilize the conventional polarization of these two aspects of the poetic. This, of course, has important implications for criticism: what then should criticism be, if it is not close reading, not 'inventorying devices' (Bernstein, 11)? Bernstein's answer is 'the criticism of desire:/ sowing not reaping'. A dynamic engagement with the work which is 'intoxicated with its own metaphoricity,/ or tropicality', ludic and transformative rather than elucidatory. This, it seems, is the paradigm for the criticism that appears – particularly in the reviews – in the journal, *L=A=N=G=U=A=G=E*.

Bernstein's 'absorption' and Forrest-Thomson's 'naturalization', though related, are not equivalent. Absorption is the primary canonical mode of that tradition in poetry which performs most of the construction of the text on the reader's behalf, so that the reader becomes a consumer of commodified experience. Bernstein defines his term by a metonymic chain of associations:

> By *absorption* I mean engrossing, engulfing
> completely, engaging, arresting attention, reverie,
> attention-intensification, rhapsodic, spellbinding,
> mesmerizing, hypnotic, total, riveting,
> enthralling: belief, conviction, silence.

> (Bernstein, 21)

His catalogue of Romantic effects and affects gets a twist in its tail from the ideological implications of the fact that 'enthralling' leads grammatically through a colon to 'belief, conviction, silence'. Bernstein's invocation of silence in the context of absorption recalls how in 'Cordelia' Forrest-Thomson draws attention to and attempts to elude the silencing of the doubly marginalized female experimental poet. At one point Bernstein remarks that for Bruce Andrews (his co-editor of $L=A=N=G=U=A=G=E$), as for Language poet Bob Perelman and Francophone Canadian linguistically investigative poet Nicole Brossard, 'the resistance to absorption is a/ political act' (Bernstein, 25–6). This is clearly the case for other Language poets, including Bernstein, in spite of his recognition that changes in historical situation and readership are capable of reversing the polarities of absorption and impermeability. The belief that a particular articulation of language in and of itself constitutes a radical political act is problematic, but it is a hallmark of at least the majority of Language writing. Anti-absorptive devices delay the reader's process of naturalization, enforce a focus on the materiality of language by resisting narrative assimilation, and are related to what the Russian Formalists called *ostranenie*, or making strange.[1]

Their concept of defamiliarization – the usual translation of *ostranenie* – is itself an inheritance from the English Romantic poets.[2] Shelley asserts in 'A Defence of Poetry' (1821) that: 'Poetry lifts the veil from the hidden beauty of the world, and makes familiar objects be as if they were not familiar'; and that 'it purges from our inward sight the film of familiarity which obscures from us the wonder of our being'.[3] The latter observation appears to be indebted to Coleridge's earlier (1817) description of Wordsworth's project in the *Lyrical Ballads*: 'to give the charm of novelty to things of every day . . . by awakening the mind's attention from the lethargy of custom',[4] in which Coleridge refers implicitly to the transforming power of poetry to clear away the obscuring 'film of familiarity'. It is worth noting again in this context that the relationship between the Romantic poets and twentieth-century linguistically investigative poets is closer than would at first appear, or than their theoretical and critical writings are at pains to suggest. As Bernstein writes, with a retranslation of *ostranenie*:

> Unfamiliarization
> is a well-tried
> antiabsorptive
> method;

(Bernstein, 48)

Bernstein's insistence on the connection between poetics and politics (not a major characteristic of Forrest-Thomson's poetics, though the textual politics of gender have their place) is one of the features that links Language writing to the preoccupations of the French *Tel Quel* poets. As Marjorie Perloff has suggested,[5] radically innovative poets in America can be seen as working in the tradition of the French avant-garde from which *Tel Quel* also sprang, part of the twentieth-century contribution to the development of that 'tradition of innovation' which Forrest-Thomson traces in *Poetic Artifice* (*PA* 125). However, the line of inheritance from the British and American innovative traditions is equally strong, and thus far Perloff has overlooked Forrest-Thomson's contribution in spite of a particular focus on artifice in *Radical Artifice*, and on Wittgenstein and contemporary poetics in *Wittgenstein's Ladder*.[6] For Forrest-Thomson the genealogy of linguistically investigative poets descends through Donne as much as Dada, and for Bernstein through the American linguistically innovative, formally active poetry of Dickinson, Zukofsky and Olson as well as the Europeans.

If she does not share Language writing's political project of social transformation, Forrest-Thomson's emphasis on poetry's potential for the re-imagination of language, as expressed in the epigraph to this book taken from *Poetic Artifice*, does place her work in a broad political context. Re-imagining language involves an active participation in changing perception, and creating the possibility of inaugurating new perceptions and forms of life. Edwin Morgan suggests that Ron Silliman wants readers who will realize 'the innate powers of language, and in particular the power of language to call a new alternative world into being' (Morgan, 5). The shock of the new, of this new kind of writing, should wake the dreamers from their dreams of consumption: as Bernstein puts it, 'the project is to wake/ us from the hypnosis of absorption' (Bernstein, 39). Like the Russian Formalist technique of defamiliarization or enstrangement, this dynamic relies on the existence of conventional or canonical

115

genres and forms (absorptive) that the antiabsorptive forms can question and disrupt. However, it is clear that for Bernstein – as for the Formalists with defamiliarization – absorption and impermeability, like the designations 'canonical' and 'innovative', are historically and contextually contingent. Indeed Bernstein identifies occasions on which antiabsorptive devices may paradoxically be used in the service of absorption, and gives a performative instance in which Forrest-Thomson's terms are also employed as glosses on his own argument:

> There is, then, a considerable history
> of using antiabsorptive techniques
> (nontransparent or non-'naturalizing' elements)
> (artifice)
> for absorptive
> ends. This is an approach
> I find myself peculiarly
> attracted to, & which reflects my
> ambivolence
> about absorption & its converses.

> (Bernstein, 37–8)

Bernstein uses a range of techniques here to represent his theoretical position. Varying line lengths focus attention on the two isolated words, and the first, '(artifice)', gets an additional signification from being sealed in parentheses. In addition, the idiosyncratic italicization of the 'o' in 'ambivolence' highlights the textuality of the word and helps us to recall the dual meanings of *voler* in French of 'to steal' and 'to fly' that Cixous made familiar when she suggested that: 'To fly/steal is woman's gesture, to steal into language to make it fly'.[7] Bernstein thus invokes stealing and flying in implicit apposition to value or valency (ambivalence). Whether by allusion or quotation or the more refined forms of intertextuality inherent in all forms of language, the past of language will always resonate in its present use. All our speech is a kind of stealing: flights of language are invariably made on borrowed or stolen wings. Bernstein's clever coinage also carries more than a hint of 'violence', reinforcing the sense of textual disruption, while the juxtaposition of the two parenthetical elements – both citing Forrest-Thomson – not only serves as an illustration of an antiabsorptive technique but also enacts the double movement ('antiabsorptive techniques... for absorptive ends') of Bernstein's avowed 'ambivolence' where 'absorption & its converses' are concerned.

Bernstein defines impermeability at greater length than absorption, with greater inventiveness, and with the addition of vernacular expressions that humorously counterpoint the critical terms. The repetition of 'fanciful' is particularly worth noting, calling to mind as it does another Romantic legacy: Coleridge's distinction between fancy and imagination:

> *Impermeability* suggests artifice, boredom,
> exaggeration, attention scattering, distraction,
> digression, interruptive, transgressive,
> undecorous, anticonventional, unintegrated, fractured,
> fragmented, fanciful, ornately stylized, rococo,
> baroque, structural, mannered, fanciful, ironic,
> iconic, schtick, camp, diffuse, decorative,
> repellent, inchoate, programmatic, didactic,
> theatrical, background muzak, amusing: skepticism,
> doubt, noise, resistance.
>
> (Bernstein, 21–2)

While we might expect Bernstein to focus on antiabsorption in terms of a radical poetics, his argument is more nuanced than a simple polarization, in spite of the contrasting list of synonyms. Absorptive and antiabsorptive are not articulated as contraries: 'these terms/ should not be understood as mutually exclusive,/ morally coded, or even conceptually separable' (Bernstein, 16). Rather he configures them as 'copresent/ in any method of reading or writing, although/ one or the other may be more obtrusive or evasive'. Bernstein images the potential dialectic of the interrelationship of absorption and its converse using a phrase that echoes Forrest-Thomson's ambiguous employment of the word 'prevent' in 'Sonnet' (*CP* 91):

> the absorbed & unabsorbed cleave,
> since *cleave* means both to divide
> & to hold together.
>
> (Bernstein, 16)

Again he uses line endings and italicization as part of an attempt to use poetic artifice to performatively construct a dynamic on the page.

Bernstein refuses the temptation to create new critical categories into which texts can be divided, seeming as much concerned with breaking down the distinctions between the terms he has set up, as with defining them. His emphasis is on creating the possibility of thinking about the implications of these dynamics he calls absorption and impermeability, rather than assigning texts to one or the other modality:

> To speak of a radically impervious text
> is to speak oxymoronically – absorbency and repellency
> are relative, contextual, & interpenetrating
> terms, not new critical analytic categories.
> The unreadable text is an outer limit for poetry;
>
> (Bernstein, 47)

And if we consign the aesthetic to oblivion, the utterly unreadable text is what we end up with.

At the beginning of *Artifice of Absorption* Bernstein attempts, in a minor miracle of compression, to define poem, meaning, artifice, experience, reference, and the role of the reader. Many of the key terms and concepts are familiar from Forrest-Thomson's work. By invoking the poetic as a possible attribute of reading as well as writing, Bernstein raises both the long-standing problem of defining 'a poem', and the question of the location of poetic meaning. At the same time, he asserts the significance of the writer in terms of her/his practice of artifice, which involves the resistance to reference characteristic of Language writing ('"artifice" is the contradiction of "realism"', and realism assumes a ready translatability from words to world). And in terms of her/his 'specific design' – intendedly a more forceful and ideologically less problematic way of discussing authorial intention – for the piece to be read as a poem:

> The reason it is difficult to talk about
> the meaning of a poem – in a way that doesn't seem
> frustratingly superficial or partial – is that by
> designating a text a poem, one suggests that its
> meanings are to be located in some 'complex' be-
> yond an addition of devices & subject matters.
> A poetic *reading* can be given to any
> piece of writing; a 'poem' may be understood as
> writing specifically designed to absorb, or inflate
> with, proactive – rather than reactive – styles of

118

reading. 'Artifice' is a measure of a poem's
intractability to being read as the sum of its
devices & subject matters. In this sense,
'artifice' is the contradiction of 'realism', with
its insistence on presenting an unmediated
(immediate) experience of facts, either of the
'external' world of nature or the 'internal' world
of the mind; for example, naturalistic
representation or phenomenological consciousness
mapping. Facts in poetry are primarily
factitious.

(Bernstein, 6)

If a theorist desires to retain any concept of the experience of
poetry as intersubjective – and if not, why write for any other
reader? – meaning cannot be relinquished, any more than
reference. The concept of poetry as knowledge, as 'epistemolo-
gical/ inquiry' (Bernstein, 12), equally requires an insistence on
meaning: her powerful engagement with the question of how
poems mean rather than what they mean makes Forrest-
Thomson's poetics an important contribution to the develop-
ment of postmodern poetry in the tradition of innovation, as
Bernstein is aware.

Bernstein refuses to view the designation of aspects of poetic
language as meaningless as liberatory. That would cede ground
that is far too significant; and here his argument reconnects
with Empson's and Forrest-Thomson's insistence on rationality.
However, it does so at a different level, within language itself, at
the level of intertextuality:

It is just my insistence
that poetry be understood as epistemological
inquiry; to cede meaning would be to undercut
the power of poetry to reconnect us
with modes of meaning given in language

(Bernstein, 12)

Poems may not necessarily be written in the language-game of
giving information, but the kinds of poem that interest both
Forrest-Thomson and Bernstein – as the very existence of his
poem of poetics attests – are written in the language of
information. Both consider that poetry has a function, hence
their emphasis on how poems work in both theory and poetic

119

practice, though the inquiry is not separable from the poem: 'the ideas are all inside/ the process' (Bernstein, 43). For both, the epistemological function of poetry is vital, which makes intelligibility – if not ready accessibility or absorption – essential to their poems.

Bernstein's elegant formula for the inner and outer limits of poetry is based on his conceptual schema of impermeability and absorption:

> Translating Zukofsky's formula for poetry
> (lower limit, speech; upper limit, music)
> I would suggest that
> poetry has as its outer limit, impermeability
> & as its inner limit, absorption.

(Bernstein, 48)

The line endings again highlight the theme, connecting poetry and music to impermeability and absorption. All art may indeed constantly aspire to the condition of music, but for the art of speech, for poetry, a crucial aspect of its function – as 'epistemological inquiry' – is sacrificed if it should achieve that desire. And the poetry of repellence, the radically impermeable poem, will find few readers. As Jackson Mac Low remarks, 'Whatever the intentions of the authors, if the perceivers give serious attention to the works, they will – at some "level" – be finding meanings. This is what arouses and sustains their interest and sometimes moves them emotionally' (*IAT* 494). Without that intellectual and emotional movement, what would be the interest? As Forrest-Thomson remarks in *Poetic Artifice*, 'it is not entirely clear why we should want to do away with the notion that there is feeling in poetry, for we should find ourselves very quickly arguing that poetry is of no interest at all' (*PA* 19). This is an issue which also has a bearing on the reception of Language poetry.

During the 1970s, between the twin poles of the Bay area and New York, a movement – for want of a better description – developed through readings and talks, notably Bob Perelman's Talks series.[8] These were accompanied by a range of small press publications of books, and of journals mostly now defunct, such as *This*, started by Robert Grenier and Barrett Watten in 1971; *Hills*, edited by Bob Perelman, first published in 1973; and *Poetics*

Journal, started in 1982 and still edited by Lyn Hejinian and Barrett Watten. The membership of this movement – a loose association of at least partially like-minded writers – is difficult to define, but those included in Ron Silliman's important collection *In the American Tree* (1986) are a fairly representative group. Douglas Messerli's *'Language' Poetries: An Anthology* (1987), which concentrates on the poetry while Silliman includes a large section of poetics, also provides a useful selection. In addition to these, Silliman's lengthy list of the writers excluded from his collection because they are not American, not primarily poets, or because they were established 'prior to this moment in writing' (*IAT* xx), but whom he recognizes as part of the extended field of Language operations, suggests how difficult it is in practice to identify the membership.

In particular, I would draw attention to the attempts to suggest that the 'movement' has been more international than just American, and certainly there are (and arguably always were) poets working in Canada, such as Steve McCaffery (and younger figures like Lisa Robertson), and in Britain, those such as Tom Raworth and Allen Fisher, Denise Riley and Maggie O'Sullivan, whose sustained work over a similar period bears a strong relationship to that of the core group of Language writers. Geoff Ward, one of those who makes this case (in a rare acknowledgement of the achievement of Forrest-Thomson) also includes 'at the younger end, poet-scholars like Rod Mengham, and the late Veronica Forrest-Thomson, whose work anticipates much of what has happened since' (Ward, 14). However, the core group, as I have referred to it, is comprised of those who during the seventies, and beginning in San Francisco, began to collaborate and discuss their work; and as Perelman notes, 'collaborations form a significant proportion of published language writing' (Perelman, 33).

It appears that the first time the term 'Language Poetry' was used in print to describe the work of some of these writers was in 1975, in a magazine called *Alcheringa*, which published Silliman's selection of work by himself and eight other poets, including Bruce Andrews, Clark Coolidge and Robert Grenier.[9] Its use was crystallized by the title of perhaps the best known of all the journals involved in the construction of this literary movement, *L=A=N=G=U=A=G=E*. Called by Silliman 'the first American journal of poetics by and for poets' (*IAT* xvii), $L=A=N=G=U=A=G=E$ first appeared in February 1978, and was devoted to discussing poetry and poetics through essays, short pieces, and reviews. Over the following four years four volumes were produced, and *The L=A=N=G=U=A=G=E Book*, published in 1984, reprinted a selection of pieces from volumes 1–3 (*LB* x). 'The Language Sampler', edited by Charles Bernstein, appeared in *Paris Review* 86, also in 1982, and Silliman's major work of criticism, *The New Sentence*, was published in 1989.

These are some of the founding works by founding figures, but in addition to the difficulty of establishing who is part of this group, there is even less agreement on how to refer to its work. Jerome McGann uses the term '$L=A=N=G=U=A=G=E$ Writing', calling on the title of the journal, but many would reject the identification of movement with journal his formulation implies.[10] Bob Perelman – himself on everyone's list of Language poets – prefers 'language writing' (Perelman, 17), and notes that 'even the name is hard to pin down', although '"language" is always included, sometimes capitalized' (Perelman, 19). Increasingly anxieties over nomenclature have resulted in strategies such as 'so-called language poetry' or the use of scare quotes around 'Language', or even occasionally both. Thus Edwin Morgan, a poet and academic who knew Forrest-Thomson, feels the need to refer, in one of the epigraphs to this chapter, to what he calls 'the "language" poetry position' (Morgan, 5).

The anxiety attaching to the naming and defining of this body of work reflects a number of tensions. Obviously it is primarily critics who have wanted or needed a convenient label and a definition, and from the beginning there has been considerable ambivalence amongst Language writers with regard to critics and the academy. Language writing was a reaction against – and in some ways a development from – an earlier reaction (by the Black Mountain School, Beat Poets and New York School) against academicist poetry, a reaction which had in its turn been institutionally recuperated. Over the last two decades this recuperation has increasingly been the fate of Language writing itself.

A steady proliferation of academic articles and books has been devoted to poetry which was in its initiation positively anti-academic. This is of course, as Morgan remarks, 'an ancient and recurring situation: as one set of outsiders is tamed and institutionalized, another set of outsiders is required to shake the body politic and make people think again' (Morgan, 1). Even the would-be 'outsiders' have surely benefited from the wider constituency being taken up by academic critics has provided for their work, and as Vernon Shetley remarks, 'the vigorous backing of its academic supporters has made Language writing an important issue on the American poetic scene'.[11] A wider readership must be desirable for writers whose work has so explicitly political an agenda.

A substantial number of Language poets, including some of the primary figures like Perelman, Bernstein and Barrett Watten, are now university teachers, tenured faculty members. A fact which comes in for some criticism from those like Silliman who see themselves as resistant to institutionalization. At issue here is the character of Language writing as a political project grounded in a Marxist analysis of language and society. Silliman states in 'Disappearance of the Word, Appearance of the World', that 'writing (and, through writing, language)' has been subjected to

> the social dynamics of capitalism. Words not only find themselves attached to commodities, they *become* commodities and, as such, take on the 'mystical' and 'mysterious character' Marx identified as the commodity fetish: torn from any tangible connection to their human makers, they appear instead as independent objects active in a universe of similar entities, a universe prior to, and outside, any agency by a perceiving Subject. A world whose inevitability invites acquiescence. (Silliman, 8)

Thus, for Silliman, capitalism transforms the relationship between the subject and the world, particularly by transforming the relationship between language and the world.

> What happens when a language moves toward and passes into a capitalist stage of development is an anaesthetic transformation of the perceived tangibility of the word, with corresponding increases in its expository, descriptive and narrative capacities, preconditions for the invention of 'realism', the illusion of reality in capitalist thought. These developments are tied directly to the function of reference in language, which under capitalism is transformed, narrowed into referentiality. (Silliman, 10)

On this analysis the task of the poet is to make the word tangible once again, to wake readers from the anaesthetic state induced by commodification and involve them in the production of textual meaning. 'It is our sense', say Andrews and Bernstein in 'Repossessing the Word', 'that the project of poetry does not involve turning language into a commodity for consumption; instead, it involves repossessing the sign through close attention to, and active participation in, its production' (LB x).

As this quotation suggests, Language writing's Marxism tends to be filtered through poststructuralism, particularly Kristeva's connection between revolution and poetic language and Barthes's notion of the writer cleaning up language. This latter Forrest-Thomson too invokes, in discussing Pound's 'image' as an attempt through poetic artifice 'to convert the soiled language of the everyday world to a new language that will be clean' (PA 68), echoing Barthes's description of the writer in the Critical Essays as one who 'detaches a second language from the slime of primary languages afforded him by the world, history, his existence'.[12]

The Kristevan emphasis on the revolutionary potential of poetic language can seem overstated, if not actually politically naïve. Although, as Bernstein remarks in his preface to The Politics of Poetic Form, 'radically innovative poetic styles can have political meanings'[13] (my emphasis), employing those features of poetic language ('artifice') which distinguish it from other language-games cannot of itself constitute political subversion. To imagine a direct correspondence between the contestation of a certain view of subjectivity through the problematization of its construction in language and actual social change seems equally far-fetched or utopian. It is clear, though, that the commodification of language in late or globalized capitalism is an important factor in the destruction of the conditions of possibility of an avant-garde.

A younger British poet and critic, Robert Sheppard, who has taken on board Forrest-Thomson's work, and whose investment in similar theoretical perspectives to those of the Language writers has informed his own poetry and poetics, has a rather less doctrinally Marxist view of commodification and poetic language. In a piece written in 1988 and called 'The Education of Desire', Sheppard writes 'What once belonged to poetry has been stolen. Some poets don't worry about this. But it means that a lot of poetry today will look like adverts.'[14] Increasingly advertising has come to use the insights and techniques of the twentieth-century avant-garde movements from which Language writing descends, hence their rejection of the poem as commodity and project for the 'repossession of the sign', as Andrews and Bernstein term it. No longer regarded as an 'autonomous' object, the text is now read as a process, in which the reader has a vital part, and this goes hand in hand with the renegotiation of subjectivity which is also so vital a part of Forrest-Thomson's work.

5%>Although, as we have seen, there is diversity rather than consensus amongst Language writers, all might subscribe to this idea of reading/writing as a process in which both writer and reader are dynamically involved. This concept forms part of a poetics which sets out to destabilize the very notions of self (expressive), of identity (descriptive/definitive) and of subjectivity (discursive).[15] Such an approach clearly has an implicit politics, one complementary to but distinguishable from the neo-Marxist critique of the commodification of the word. Language writers use the self-reflexivity characteristic of postmodern poetry to interrogate identity in new ways. This interrogation is literal in the case of Ron Silliman's 'Sunset Debris', a text composed of a barrage of rhetorical questions which forcefully establish linguistic positions of subjectivity: 'Didn't you hope to avoid language that passed itself off as a mockup of consciousness? Didn't you suggest a formula just to get the haters of formulae pissed off? Won't you, given the chance, betray everyone?'[16] Here the reader is reminded, as Ward notes, of their fictionality as a participant in any text, a fictionality to which Forrest-Thomson also drew attention (Ward, 26, *PA* 69).

The construction of subjectivity in language always depends on a certain type of reference from words to world, and the disruption of conventional subjectivity is often accompanied in Language writing by the use of techniques to resist the process of reference from words to world through the disruption of syntax. In *Poetic Artifice* Forrest-Thomson insists that 'it is through syntax – the suggestion that a coherent proposition is being offered – that external meaning smothers words' (*PA* 113). Syntax guarantees both an origin and a destination for the sentence, constructing the subject positions of writer and reader, while 'Language work', Bruce Andrews suggests, 'resembles a creation of a community and of a world-view by a once-divided-but-now-fused Reader and Writer' (*LB* 35). The politics of syntax is explored in what is perhaps Silliman's best-known essay, 'The New Sentence', which discusses the prose poems of the Bay area. Silliman ends his essay with this paragraph from Watten's *Plasma*:

> Everywhere there are spontaneous literary discussions. Something structurally new is being referred to. These topics may be my very own dreams, which everyone takes a friendly interest in. The library extends for miles under the ground. (Silliman, 93)[17]

Silliman remarks that in such poetry 'the paragraph organizes the sentences in fundamentally the same way a stanza does lines of verse' (Silliman, 89). What he calls the 'new sentence' sustains the grammatical form of the sentence, but, by identifying 'the signifier...as the locus of literary meaning...reverses the dynamics which have so long been associated with the tyranny of the signified' (Silliman, 93). One feels that for Silliman this is more than a merely aesthetic achievement: it is 'something different, and more than, a style'. As Rod Mengham says in a similar connection, 'the analogy between syntactical conventions and structures of social control...is sharp enough'.[18]

The suggestion that Language poets have repossessed the sign by transforming the role of the reader/writer carries with it the implication that these poets have a privileged relationship to language itself. It is not surprising, then, that poets of other kinds have taken exception to this appropriation, apparently symbolized by the ascription of 'Language', or 'Language-centred', or 'linguistically innovative' (Gilbert Adair's coinage) to these writers, claiming that they too focus on language, and innovate. In his essay 'Language-Centred', first published in volume 4 of $L=A=N=G=U=A=G=E$ and collected in *In the American Tree*, Jackson Mac Low, a poet often associated with Language writing but whose work with aleatory or chance procedures predates it, problematizes that descriptive label: 'The term "language-centred" is ill chosen. The many works thrown under this rubric are no more "centred in language" than a multitude of other literary works. Many depart from normal syntax. In many, what might be called "subject matter" shifts rapidly. In some, such as many of my own, principles such as "objective hazard," "indeterminacy," and "lessening of the dominance of the ego" may predominate over more usual concerns. But that a writer's efforts are ever "centred in language" is highly dubious' (*IAT* 491).

If one accepts this analysis, then it seems possible that much of the anxiety which focuses on nomenclature reflects not only a concern that Language writing may be incorporated or absorbed into the establishment or the mainstream and hence commodified, but also the fear that the project as set out in various writings, both individual and collective, was always impossible to realize, and that any attempts to identify and discuss more than individual pieces of work will reveal the inherent problems in the '"language" poetry position'. It should by now be apparent why there is bound to be disagreement about how to discuss Language writing.

Although the Language poets have never produced a manifesto as such, they have written extensively about poetics. Most criticism of Language writing has concerned itself with how closely (or not) the writings bear out their writers' intentions for them. Perloff remarks in *Radical Artifice* (1991) that with a new 'movement' critics are dependent to some extent on the practitioners' own accounts of their practice in order to orient themselves to this new, this unfamiliar phenomenon.[19] (Although it is hard to see that Language writing was really new at this point, even if relatively new to academic critics – in fact Perelman suggests in *The Marginalization of Poetry* (1996) that 'the initial phase of language writing is over' (Perelman, 17).) Of course the Language poets' own prolific output of talks and writings about their works, which in principle are not intended to be separable from 'the work' itself – part of their contestation of the bifurcation of criticism or theory and practice – invites this approach. Reliance on poets' analyses may be tempting, but poets tend to be radically unreliable narrators when it comes to their own work. Literary criticism, too, is a long way from the (pre-New Criticism) period in which a primary concern with authorial intentionality informed analysis. When was the political or aesthetic project even as formally outlined in a manifesto ever fulfilled by the practice? Such writings are best read as taking aim, setting a trajectory.

In addition to the criticism which discusses Language writing as a whole, some of it produced by Language poets themselves, Language writers, in evaluations of the work of their associates, produce criticism of a very different kind: reviews in '$L=A=N=G=U=A=G=E$' are notably reactive and citational. This is a process Bernstein calls 'the criticism of desire:/ sowing not reaping' (Bernstein, 11). Academic critics, by contrast, have produced interesting work focussed on what individual writings 'mean', even though this cuts against the grain of the writers' own primary concern with how meaning is produced. This criticism has mostly relied upon an elucidation of Language writing's frequently strange juxtapositions, use of non sequiturs, and coinages, in terms of the already-known (analogous words or constructions), or already-written (close readings which explore their citations or deformed quotations from previous works, usually canonical). Some of these close readings are remarkably resourceful, including those of Perloff, whose 'The Word as Such: $L=A=N=G=U=A=G=E$ Poetry in the Eighties',[20] first published in *American Poetry Review* in 1984, has been a useful source and provocation for subsequent writers.

It is no coincidence that Lyn Hejinian is probably the most widely read and appreciated of the Language writers: Ward calls *My Life* 'everyone's favourite Language book' (Ward 12), and suggests that what he calls *My Life*'s 'attractively patterned reminiscence' is 'easier to take' than much Language writing. Certainly Hejinian's use of repetition, and indebtedness to the work of Gertrude Stein – an important precursor of Language poetry, as Silliman indicates in 'The New Sentence' – render the new sentences of this work more accessible than, say, some of the more energetically fragmented and dislocated Language writing. But what Ward reads as 'attractively patterned reminiscence' seems to Robert Sheppard 'only ironically a personal discourse, since "my life" is conducted primarily at the level of form, not of content'.[21] I suggest that, as in the work of Forrest-Thomson, it is impossible entirely to separate the two in Hejinian's intensely pleasurable and intellectually engaging text. Theory and work are commingled by an intercutting of self-reflexive commentary throughout the work, frequently blurring the distinction between the two categories:

There is so little public beauty. I found myself dependent on a pause, a rose, something on paper. It is a way of saying, I want you, too, to have this experience, so that we are more alike, so that we are closer, bound together, sharing a point of view – so that we are 'coming from the same place.' It is possible to be homesick in one's own neighborhood. Afraid of the bears. (Hejinian, 21–2)

As Hejinian herself remarks in 'The Rejection of Closure', 'form is not a fixture but an activity'.[22] That is, it is not static but dynamic. In *My Life*, Hejinian is engaged in redefining what narrative can be, particularly 'autobiographical' narrative, emphasizing the process of writing rather than writing as an object to be interpreted. Like Bernstein's and Forrest-Thomson's, this is work towards the construction of a poetics of writing.

My Life alternately invites and resists recuperation, and makes use of absorption and impermeability by turns, at the level of syntax as well as narrative. This is an interrupted and at times dyschronic narrative which occasionally adheres to and frequently departs from conventional expectations, especially expectations of an 'autobiographical' piece. As Perloff notes,[23] Hejinian juxtaposes 'The sweet aftertaste of artichokes' and 'The lobes of autobiography' (Hejinian, 21). This autobiography is, like the artichoke, something that if consumed unwarily could prove seriously indigestible: 'The artichoke has done its best, armoured, with scales, barbed, and hiding in its interior the soft hairs so aptly called the choke' (Hejinian, 47).

An early sentence tantalizingly evokes 'An "oral history" on paper' (Hejinian, 8). And indeed at times we seem to hear a range of speaking voices, the main narrator, ventriloquizing fragmentary phrases and stories from other related lives, some proverbial: 'Pretty is as pretty does' (Hejinian, 7), others more readily attributable to an identifiable figure: 'I'm not your maid I'm your mother' (Hejinian, 28). The autobiographical is indeed undercut by a prevailing tone of gentle irony, but not altogether displaced by it. Partly at least the effect is a product of the form, which Ward describes as 'a collage of what are arguably non sequiturs' (Ward, 30). It is also often the irony inseparable from a retrospective construction of a younger self: 'Now that I was "old enough to make my own decisions," I dressed like everyone else' (Hejinian, 36).

The first version of *My Life* was published in 1980 and consisted of thirty-seven paragraphs of thirty-seven sentences, one of each for every year of Hejinian's life. A later version, the most widely available, published in 1987, is of forty-five paragraphs of forty-five sentences: eight new sentences were added to existing paragraphs, and eight new paragraphs added to the whole.[24] Each paragraph, made up of sentences from one word to several phrases long (some are grammatically complete – occasionally inverted – others very much not; apparently rhetorical questions routinely appear without question marks), is introduced, if not quite entitled, by an italicized phrase set in an indentation in the text. This phrase makes links through repetition (with variations) in the text. The brief biography at the end of the second version of *My Life* tells us that Hejinian first used this device in the earlier *Gesauldo*, which was published in the same year as her *Writing is an Aid to Memory*[25] (Hejinian, 116).

Perhaps the most striking example of the technique is the first phrase of the text, *'A pause, a rose, something on paper'*, which is followed by the words 'A moment yellow...' (Hejinian, 7). Perloff suggests that 'It is the poet herself who is pausing to put "something on paper," something that is her written offering, her "rose"'.[26] And certainly, at a later stage in the text, Hejinian writes 'And if I feel like a book, a person on paper, I will continue' (Hejinian, 76). However, in an essay 'Variations: A Return of Words' (*IAT* 503–9), Hejinian writes 'What is possibly my earliest recollection is of a brilliantly yellow flower sharp on the grass. From that period also come other purely visual memories. I remember clearly particular wallpapers, the small yellow roses on the yellowing paper in my grandmother's room' (*IAT* 507). The memory, at once sharp and specific, of a yellow flower, of yellow roses on yellow paper, becomes in *My Life* both thematic (recurrent) and diffused into 'a rose, something on paper', and 'a moment yellow' where the inversion of moment and yellow places the emphasis on the adjective, the yellowness, rather than the noun, the moment.

This memory written down, part of the content of the text, by repetition becomes part of the structure, the form. It also recalls Stein's own brilliant defamiliarization of the red rose of romance and lyric, 'A rose is a rose is a rose is a rose', of which she said 'I think that in that line the rose is red [without colour being mentioned] for the first time in English poetry for a hundred years'.[27] Further into *My Life* Hejinian writes that 'The symbolism of the rose depends on its purity of color', and that 'The red rose in its redness leaks no yellow' (Hejinian, 65), linking intensity of colour and redness, to the exclusion of yellow, in a way that unmistakably links Stein's rose to the opening of *My Life*. The repetitions, with and without variations, work, as the narrator reflects, 'as when one repeats a word or phrase over and over in order to disintegrate its associations, to defamiliarize it' (Hejinian, 113). Also in 'Variations: A Return of Words', Hejinian notes that 'It is in rereading one's journals, especially the old ones, that one discovers the repetition of certain concerns, the recurrence of certain issues, certain chronic themes that are one's own' (*IAT* 503). 'A pause, a rose, something on paper' provides the tracery of one of these themes that keep the reader connected, intellectually and affectively, to *My Life*: to what the narrator evocatively calls 'the wobble of the rough circles of a self' (Hejinian, 42).

Language poetry has been characterized as affectless, or atonal, but in Hejinian's work – and in that of other Language writers – we find a similar capacity of thought to pierce us that Forrest-Thomson's poems so powerfully explore. If we are indeed 'language   Lost/ in language' as Susan Howe suggests in one of the epigraphs to this book, then it is also in language that we may be found.

Notes

PROLOGUE

1. Shoshana Felman, 'To Open the Question', in *Literature and Psychoanalysis. The Question of Reading: Otherwise*, Yale French Studies 55/56 (1977), 5.

CHAPTER 1. *IDENTI-KIT*

1. John Keats's letter to George and Tom Keats, 22 December 1817, 'Letter 32', in *The Letters of John Keats*, 4th edn (London: Oxford University Press, 1952), 69–72 (71).
2. Although the footnotes to her discussion of the poem and Empson's reading are inaccurate. It would seem that she confused two essays of Empson's, both in the *Kenyon Review*. The first, 'Donne and the Rhetorical Tradition', is in 11 (1949) (571–87); the second, 'Donne the Spaceman', is in 19 (1957), 337–99, and is the one to which she wrongly attributes the quotations.
3. 'A Retrospect', in T. S. Eliot (ed.), *Literary Essays of Ezra Pound* (London: Faber and Faber, 1954), 3.
4. J. Laplanche and J.-B. Pontalis, *The Language of Psycho-Analysis*, trans. Donald Nicholson-Smith (London: Hogarth Press and Institute of Psycho-Analysis, 1983), 255.
5. Edwin Morgan, review of *Identi-kit*, in *Tlaloc*, 15, published 13 July 1967, from Box 1: Miscellaneous Documents, Publisher's File of Record Copies, in the Cavan McCarthy 'Tlaloc Archive', Poetry Library, University College London. The pages of *Tlaloc* were not numbered.
6. Andrew Marvell, 'The Garden', in *The Poems and Letters of Andrew Marvell*, vol. 1, *Poems*, ed. H. M. Margoliouth (Oxford: Clarendon, 1927), 48–50 (49).
7. Castor and Pollux, sons of Leda, at the same birth as Helen and Clytemnestra; see Robert Graves, *The Greek Myths*, vol. 1

(Harmondsworth: Penguin, 1957), 246. Polydeuces and Helen were the children of Zeus in the guise of a swan; Castor and Clytemnestra the children of Leda's husband Tyndareus: thus they are children of two fathers, born of one mother.

CHAPTER 2: *LANGUAGE-GAMES*

1. My thanks to Isobel Armstrong for this information.
2. The reference following the colon is to the proposition number.
3. David Pears, *Wittgenstein* (London: Fontana, 1985), 138.
4. Sappho, *Sappho and the Greek Lyric Poets*, trans. and annotated by Willis Barnstone (New York: Schocken, 1972), 276. This edition was revised and expanded from *Greek Lyric Poetry* (New York: Bantam, 1962).
5. *Sappho*, 126, p. 67.
6. Peter Nicholls, *Modernisms: A Literary Guide* (Basingstoke: Macmillan, 1995), 129.
7. *Sappho*, p. 268.
8. My thanks to Kate Perry, Archivist of Girton College, for alerting me to this.
9. Ludwig Wittgenstein, *Tractatus Logico-Philosophicus* (London: Routledge & Kegan Paul, 1985), 149: 5:6.
10. Cristopher Nash, *World-Games: The Tradition of Anti-Realist Revolt* (London: Methuen, 1987), 233.
11. Pears, *Wittgenstein*, 13.
12. Pears, *Wittgenstein*, 13.
13. Jonathan Culler has suggested to me that the last two lines may refer to Chomsky's celebrated 'colorless green ideas sleep furiously', which she also quoted at the Cambridge Poetry Festival, 18 April 1975. Culler also informs me that the title of 'It Doesn't Matter about Mantrippe' was a phrase Forrest-Thomson overhead him use in reference to a student of his.
14. Ernst Gombrich, *Art and Illusion: A Study in the Psychology of Pictorial Representation* (New York: Pantheon, 1960), 5. Veronica Forrest-Thomson, 'Rational Artifice: Some Remarks on the Poetry of William Empson', *Yearbook of English Studies*, 4 (1974), 225–38 (231).
15. Gombrich, *Art and Illusion*, 5–6.
16. Ezra Pound, 'A Retrospect', in T. S. Eliot (ed.), *Literary Essays of Ezra Pound* (London: Faber and Faber, 1985), 3–14 (4). My thanks to Helen Carr for our discussion of Pound's usage.
17. Raman Selden, *A Reader's Guide to Contemporary Literary Theory* (Hemel Hempstead: Harvester Wheatsheaf, 1985), 114.

18. Barrett Watten, 'New Meaning and Poetic Vocabulary: From Coleridge to Jackson Mac Low', in *Poetics Today*, 18:2 (1997), 147–86 (148).
19. Roland Barthes, *Writing Degree Zero & Elements of Semiology*, trans. Annette Lavers and Colin Smith (London: Cape, 1984), 16–17.

CHAPTER 3. *ON THE PERIPHERY*

1. As quoted (unreferenced) by Annette Lavers as the title for chapter 12 of her *Roland Barthes: Structuralism and After* (London: Methuen, 1982), 167.
2. Archibald MacLeish, *New & Collected Poems 1917–1976* (Boston: Houghton Miflin, 1976), 106–7 (106).
3. Roland Barthes, *Writing Degree Zero & Elements of Semiology*, trans. Annette Lavers and Colin Smith (London: Cape, 1984), 16–17.
4. Jacques Lacan, *Écrits : A Selection*, trans. Alan Sheridan (London: Tavistock, 1977), 154.
5. My thanks to Jonathan Culler for locating the quotation.
6. Frances Cornford, 'To a Fat Lady Seen From the Train: Triolet', in Fleur Adcock (ed.), *The Faber Book of 20th Century Women's Poetry* (London: Faber, 1987), 33.
7. For example in Susan Howe, 'Secret History of the Dividing Line', in *Frame Structures: Early Poems 1974–1979* (New York: New Directions, 1996), 116 and 122.
8. William Empson, *Collected Poems* (London: Chatto and Windus, 1955), 113.
9. Roland Barthes, *S/Z* (Paris: Seuil, 1970), 227.
10. My thanks to Jonathan Culler for helping me to correct both Forrest-Thomson's French and my own!
11. Jonathan Culler, *Barthes* (London: Fontana, 1990), 58.
12. Wallace Stevens, *The Collected Poems of Wallace Stevens* (London: Faber and Faber, 1984), 429–30 (429). Forrest-Thomson quotes the couplet 'Natives of poverty, children of malheur,/ The gaiety of language is our seigneur', from Stevens, 'Esthétique du Mal', *Collected Poems*, 313–26 (322), as one of the epigraphs to her 'Necessary Artifice: Form and Theory in the Poetry of *Tel Quel*', *Language and Style*, 6:1 (1973), 3–26 (3); and Culler quotes 'gaiety of language is our seigneur' (SP 187). Culler also quotes 'The poem must resist the intelligence/ Almost successfully' (SP 178), from Stevens, 'Man Carrying Thing', *Collected Poems*, 350–1 (350); and Forrest-Thomson uses the same quotation as the epigraph to her 'Irrationality and Artifice: A Problem in Recent Poetics', *British Journal of Aesthetics*, 2 (1971), 123–33 (123). Neither gives a reference.

13. Especially as she bought a house in Birmingham, which her brother tells me was in a poor state of repair.
14. William Empson, 'Obscurity and Annotation', in John Haffenden (ed.), *Argufying: Essays on Literature and Culture* (London: Hogarth Press, 1988), 70–87 (86).
15. Anthony Rudolph, *Poems for Shakespeare*, 4 (London: Globe Playhouse Publications, 1976). The edition is dedicated 'To the memory of Veronica Forrest-Thomson', who died the day she was due to give her reading at the event this edition commemorates.
16. A notebook of work in progress is entitled 'Pomes'.
17. William Shakespeare, *King Richard II*, The Arden Shakespeare (London: Methuen, 1961), Act V, scene v, pp. 169–73 (169).
18. *Richard II*, 169–70.
19. Jacques Derrida, 'Structure, Sign and Play in the Discourse of the Human Sciences', in David Lodge (ed.), *Modern Criticism and Theory* (Harlow: Longman, 1988), 108–23.

CHAPTER 4. *POETIC ARTIFICE*

1. Peter Porter, 'On the best battlefields, no dead bodies' (review of *Collected Poems and Translations*), *Observer*, 5 August 1990.
2. Gérard Genette, 'Poetic Language, Poetics of Language', in *Figures of Literary Discourse*, trans. Alan Sheridan (Oxford: Blackwell, 1982), 75–102 (100–1).
3. Julia Kristeva, *Revolution in Poetic Language*, trans. Margaret Waller (New York, Columbia University Press, 1984).
4. Jonathan Culler analyses Kristeva's practice and establishes decisively that in her textual analyses she encompasses both interpretations (Culler2, 100–18).
5. Roland Barthes, *Image Music Text*, trans. Stephen Heath (London: Fontana, 1977), 142–8 (142).
6. Julia Kristeva, *Semiotiké: Recherches pour une sémanalyse* (Paris: Seuil, 1969).
7. A relationship between Barthes and Kristeva that Culler notes in *Structuralist Poetics*, 139–40.
8. Isobel Armstrong, *Victorian Poetry: Poetry, Poetics and Politics* (London: Routledge, 1993), 12.
9. J. Laplanche and J.-B. Pontalis, *The Language of Psycho-Analysis*, trans. Donald Nicholson-Smith (London: Hogarth Press and the Institute of Psycho-Analysis, 1983), 356.
10. Culler notes: 'poems containing questions explicitly assert their intertextual nature, not just because they seem to request an answer and hence designate themselves as incomplete, but

because the presuppositions carried by their questions imply a prior discourse' (Culler2, 113).

11. William Empson, *Some Versions of Pastoral: A Study of the Pastoral Form in Literature* (Harmondsworth: Penguin, 1966), 77–85.

12. Perhaps the poem was written in a British Rail Services 'refreshment room'; in any case the dedication (not italicized in *Cordelia*) calls to mind the film *Brief Encounter*.

13. Occitan is frequently the currently preferred designation, as the *langue d'oc* was spoken over a larger area of southern medieval France than Provence, but both are acceptable.

14. Christopher Marlowe, *The Jew of Malta* (c. 1592), ed. N. W. Bawcutt (Manchester: Manchester University Press, 1978), Act 4, scene 1, pp. 148–9:
    BARNARDINE: Thou has committed –
    BARABAS: Fornication? But that was in another country: and besides, the wench is dead.

15. Dante Alighieri, *The Comedy of Dante Alighieri the Florentine, Cantica II: Purgatory*, trans. Dorothy L. Sayers (Harmondsworth: Penguin, 1955), Canto 26, 1. 117, p. 275. According to the note on p. 279 of this edition, 'Petrarch agrees with Dante's estimate, and calls him [Arnaut] "the great master of love".'

16. Arnaut Daniel, *Le Canzoni di Arnaut Daniel*, 2 vols, ed. Maurizio Perugi (Milan: Ricciardi, 1978), vol. II, p. 497. Perugi's version of 'Canzone XV' differs slightly from that in Canello's earlier edition, as used by Pound: Ugo A. Canello, *La Vita e le opere del trovatore Arnaldo Daniello* (Halle: Niemeyer, 1883). My thanks to Claire Marshall and Ian Short of Birkbeck College for helping me to check the language here, and to Ian Short for this close translation.

17. James J. Wilhelm, *Il Miglior Fabbro: The Cult of the Difficult in Daniel, Dante, and Pound* (Orono, ME: National Poetry Foundation, University of Maine at Orono, 1982), 12.

18. Ezra Pound, 'Arnaut Daniel', in *Literary Essays*, 110.

19. Ezra Pound, *Translations* (Norfolk, CT: New Directions, 1963), 178–81.

20. Pound, *Translations*, 179.

21. In her *Pomes* notebook, 'In Memoriam' is dedicated to the still very much alive Jonathan Culler; this was later changed to 'for W. S. Gilbert'.

22. Wilhelm, *Il Miglior Fabbro*, 10.

23. Daniel, *Le Canzoni*, 333.

24. Pound, *Translations*, 423.

25. Pound, *Translations*, 423–4.

26. Forrest-Thomson's reference reads: 'Quoted by M. Hartmann, *Das*

arabische Stropengedicht (Frankfurt, 1905), pp. 100–101' (*PA* 167 n. 20).

27. In a conversation with me in London on 8 November 1995.

28. As cited by Peter Brooks in his introduction to Tzvetan Todorov, *Introduction to Poetics*, trans. Richard Howard (Minneapolis: University of Minnesota Press, 1981).

29. Empson, *Pastoral*, 19. Empson extends the term to include any work of literature in which an idealized, usually more morally wholesome, world is depicted.

30. Empson, *Pastoral*, 25.

31. The punctuation in *Cordelia* is different, and shifts the meaning: 'creatures' clover'. This permits both the interpretation of 'our creatures' as 'in clover', or that the 'clover' – a livestock foodstuff – is fodder for 'our creatures' (*C* 18). Barnett has very reasonably accepted the later *On the Periphery* punctuation (Cambridge, Street Editions, 1976, p. 30), but the earlier variant is both interesting, and quite plausible.

32. My thanks to Jonathan Culler for sending me copies of annotated typescripts, including this, together with a copy of the *Pomes* notebook.

33. It is tempting but not necessary to suggest (as Simon Perril does) that this may be the result of a typographical error: 'Contemporary British Poetry and Modernist Invention (unpublished PhD thesis, Cambridge, 1995), 106. Jonathan Culler thinks Perril may be right, considering the messy state of the *Poetic Artifice* typescript. However, in his fine 'Personal Memoir', J. H. Prynne comes close to confirming the published text when he remarks that 'the physical properties of speech always bothered her' (*On the Periphery*, 43).

34. Thomas Mann, *Doctor Faustus: The Life of the German Composer Adrian Leverkühn as Told by a Friend* (London: Secker & Warburg, 1976), 241.

35. John Donne, 'The Sunne Rising', in *The Poems of John Donne*, ed. H. J. C. Grierson (London: Oxford University Press/Humphry Milford, 1929), 10–11.

36. John Haffenden, *Novelists in Interview* (London: Methuen, 1985), 82.

37. My thanks to Helen Carr for reminding me of this.

38. Bice Benvenuto and Roger Kennedy, *The Works of Jacques Lacan: An Introduction* (London: Free Association Books, 1986), 119.

39. Linda Hutcheon, *Irony's Edge: The Theory and Politics of Irony* (London: Routledge, 1994), 50.

40. W. B. Yeats, *The Poems: A New Edition*, ed. Richard J. Finneran (London: Macmillan, 1984), 193–4 (193).

CODA: *CORDELIA*

1. Harold Bloom, *The Anxiety of Influence: A Theory of Poetry* (New York: Oxford University Press, 1973).
2. British Library National Sound Archive T6013WR.
3. William Shakespeare, *The Tempest*, The Arden Edition of the Works of William Shakespeare, ed. Frank Kermode (London: Methuen, 1964), Act I, scene ii, p. 35.
4. 'Prince Possum', in 'Tradition and the Individual Talent'.
5. In Susan Howe, *The Europe of Trusts* (Los Angeles: Sun & Moon Press, 1990), 170–80 and 183–217.
6. W. C. Sellar and R. J. Yeatman, *1066 and All That, a Memorable History of England, Comprising All the Parts You Can Remember, Including 103 Good Things, 5 Bad Things, and 2 Genuine Dates* (Harmondsworth: Penguin/Methuen, 1960).
7. The opening line to the 'General Prologue' to *The Canterbury Tales*; Geoffrey Chaucer, *The Works of Chaucer*, ed. F. N. Robinson (London: Oxford University Press, 1957), 17–25 (17).
8. Archibald MacLeish: *New & Collected Poems 1917–1976* (Boston: Houghton Miflin, 1976), 106–7.
9. Philip Davies Roberts, *How Poetry Works: The Elements of English Poetry* (Harmondsworth: Penguin, 1976), 78.

CHAPTER 5. LANGUAGE, LANGUAGE, L=A=N=G=U=-A=G=E

1. Introduction to Victor Shklovsky's essay, 'Art as Technique', in *Russian Formalist Criticism: Four Essays*, trans. Lee. T. Lemon and Marion J. Reis (Lincoln: University of Nebraska Press, 1965), 3.
2. As noted in Chris Baldick, *Concise Dictionary of Literary Terms* (Oxford: Oxford University Press, 1990), 54.
3. Percy Bysshe Shelley, 'A Defence of Poetry', in *Shelley's Literary and Philosophical Criticism*, ed. John Shawcross (London: Frowde, 1909), 120–59 (131 and 156).
4. Samuel Taylor Coleridge, *Biographia Literaria or Biographical Sketches of my Literary Life and Opinions* (London: Dent, 1956), 169.
5. Marjorie Perloff, *The Poetics of Indeterminacy: Rimbaud to Cage* (Princeton: Princeton University Press, 1981).
6. Marjorie Perloff, *Radical Artifice: Writing Poetry in the Age of Media* (Chicago: University of Chicago Press, 1991); Perloff, *Wittgenstein's Ladder: Poetic Language and the Strangeness of the Ordinary* (Chicago: University of Chicago Press, 1996).

7. Hélène Cixous and Catherine Clément, *The Newly Born Woman*, trans. Betsy Wing (Manchester: Manchester University Press, 1986), 96. See also Claudine Herrmann, *Les Voleuses de langue* (Paris: Des Femmes, 1979).

8. Some are published in *Talks* (*Hills*, 6/7), and *Writing/Talks* (Carbondale: Southern Illinois University Press, 1985), both edited by Bob Perelman.

9. Lee Bartlett, 'What is "Language Poetry"?', *Critical Inquiry*, 12 (Summer 1986), 741–52 (742). See also Ward, 14.

10. 'Contemporary Poetry, Alternate Routes', *Politics and Poetic Value*, ed. Robert van Hallberg (Chicago: University of Chicago Press, 1987), 253–76 (253).

11. Vernon Shetley, 'The Return of the Repressed: Language Poetry and the New Formalism', *After the Death of Poetry: Poet and Audience in Contemporary America* (Durham, NC: Duke University Press, 1993), 135–64 (137).

12. Roland Barthes, *Critical Essays*, trans. Richard Howard (Evanston, IL: Northwestern University Press, 1972), xvii.

13. *The Politics of Poetic Form: Poetry and Public Policy*, ed. Charles Bernstein (New York: Roof Books, 1990), vii.

14. Originally written for his A level students (mostly 16–18 years old), and reprinted in his *Far Language: Poetics and Linguistically Innovative Poetry 1978–1997* (Exeter: Stride, 1999), 28–30 (28).

15. In an e-mail message to me of 25 July 1998 Barrett Watten writes 'there is a wide gulf between self and "subject," the former being expressive and the latter discursive'.

16. Ron Silliman, *The Age of Huts* (New York: Roof, 1986), 32, as cited by Ward, 26.

17. Barrett Watten, 'Plasma', in *Plasma/Parallels/"X"* (Berkeley: Tuumba Press, 1979), no pagination.

18. Rod Mengham, untitled review of five Language texts in *Textual Practice*, 3:1 (1989), 115–24 (122).

19. Perloff, *Radical Artifice*, 173.

20. Reprinted in Perloff, *The Poetics of Indeterminacy: Rimbaud to Cage* (Princeton: Princeton University Press, 1981), 215–38.

21. Robert Sheppard, 'Elsewhere and Everywhere: Other New (British) Poetries', *Critical Survey*, 10:1 (1998), 17–32 (27).

22. *Writing/Talks*, ed. Bob Perelman (Carbondale: Southern Illinois University Press, 1985), 270–91 (275).

23. Marjorie Perloff, '"The sweet taste of artichokes, the lobes of autobiography": Lyn Hejinian's *My Life*', *fragmente*, 2 (1990), 49–56.

24. A section of a version for the nineties appears in *Out of Everywhere: Linguistically Innovative Poetry by Women in North America & the UK*,

ed. Maggie O'Sullivan (London: Reality Street Editions, 1996), 63–5.

25. Lyn Hejinian, *Writing is an Aid to Memory* (Berkeley: The Figures, 1978/Los Angeles: Sun & Moon Press, 1996).
26. Perloff, *Radical Artifice*, 167.
27. Gertrude Stein, 'Poetry and Grammar', in *Look at Me Now and Here I am: Writings and Lectures 1909–45*, ed. Patricia Meyerowitz (Harmondsworth: Penguin, 1990), 7, n. 1, reads 'Quoted by Thornton Wilder in his introduction to *Four in America*'.

Select Bibliography

WORKS BY VERONICA FORREST-THOMSON

As Veronica Forrest

'The Room', *Equator*, 2 [1966].
Identi-kit (London: Outposts, 1967).
'The White Magician'; 'Computer 97/100DV'; 'Literary Historian'; *Continuum*, 5 [1967?], 8, 27, 30.
Contributor's note and 4 poems: 'Fêtes Nationales & Zazie in the London Underground'; 'The Blue Book'; 'Letters of Ezra Pound'; 'Epitaph for an Unnamed Priestess', *Solstice*, 9 (1969), 3, 20–4.
twelve academic questions (Cambridge: The Author, 1970).
'Habitat', in *Tlaloc*, 15 (1967).
'Silver Escalator', from '2 Staircase Poems', in *Tlaloc*, 17 (1968).
With Cavan McCarthy, *Veronicavan: Program of a Reading at the Bristol Arts Centre*, 30 December 1967.

As Veronica Forrest-Thomson

Collections
Language-Games (Leeds: School of English Press, University of Leeds, 1971).
Cordelia or 'A poem should not mean but be' ([Leicester]: Omens, 1974).
On the Periphery (Cambridge: Street Editions, 1976).
Collected Poems and Translations, ed. Anthony Barnett (London: Allardyce, Barnett, 1990).
Selected Poems, ed. Anthony Barnett (London: Invisible Books, forthcoming).

Poetics
'Poetry as Knowledge: The Use of Science by Twentieth-Century Poets' (unpublished doctoral thesis, University of Cambridge, 1971).
Poetic Artifice: A Theory of Twentieth-Century Poetry (Manchester:

Manchester University Press, 1978).

Articles

'Irrationality and Artifice: A Problem in Recent Poetics', *British Journal of Aesthetics*, 2 (1971), 123–33.

'Au-delà du Réel: La Poésie anglaise moderne à l'heure du choix', trans. Michel Canavaggio, *Chroniques de l'art vivant*, 29 (1972), 24–5.

'Beyond Reality: Orders of Possibility in Modern English Poetry', *Fuse*, 1 (1972), 20–3.

'Levels in Poetic Convention', *Journal of European Studies*, 2 (1972), 35–51.

'The Ritual of Reading *Salammbô*', *Modern Language Review*, 67 (1972), 787–98.

'Necessary Artifice: Form and Theory in the Poetry of *Tel Quel*', *Language and Style*, 6:1 (1973), 3–26.

'Dada, Unrealism and Contemporary Poetry', *20th Century Studies*, 12 (1974), 77–93.

'Rational Artifice: Some Remarks on the Poetry of William Empson', *Yearbook of English Studies*, 4 (1974), 225–38.

'Unrealism as the Poetic Mode for This Century', *Spindrift*, 1 ([1977?]), 16–27.

'La Planète séparée: John Donne et William Empson', trans. François Maguin, in *John Donne*, Cahiers de l'Herne: Les Dossiers H (Paris: l'Age d'Homme, 1983), 213–44.

Poems and Extracts from Other Works

Typed extract from letter to Adrian Flick, 7 May 1972, and three poems: 'L'effet du réel'; 'On Naming of Shadows'; 'Selection Restrictions on Peanuts for Dinner'; in *Landseer*, 1:3 (1972), 2–3.

'Richard II', in *Poems for Shakespeare*, 4, ed. Anthony Rudolph (London: Globe Playhouse Publications, 1976), 24–5.

'Poems of Youth', *Adam International Review*, 391–3 (1975), 46–9.

'A Letter to GS Fraser', *Adam International Review*, 391–3 (1975), 49–50.

'Sonnet', in Wendy Mulford and others (eds), *The Virago Book of Love Poetry* (London: Virago, 1990), 34.

'Pastoral'; 'The Lady of Shalott: Ode'; 'The Garden of Proserpine'; 'Cordelia or "A poem should not mean but be"'; 'Richard II'; in Andrew Crozier and Tim Longville (eds), *A Various Art* (London: Paladin, 1990), 117–27.

'From *Poetic Artifice*', in *Poets in Writing: Britain, 1970–1991*, ed. Denise Riley (Basingstoke: Macmillan, 1992), 222–33.

Sound Material

Reading at Essex Arts Festival, 27 April 1967: 'Through the Looking

Glass'; 'According to the Script'; 'Clown by Paul Klee'; 'Subatomic Symphony'; National Sound Archive T7209WR.

Reading at Cambridge Poetry Festival, 17 April 1975: 'The Garden of Proserpine'; 'Cordelia or "A poem should not mean but be"'; 'S/Z'; 'Lemon and Rosemary'; 'The Lady of Shalott'; 'Strike'; National Sound Archive T6013WR.

Poetry Forum: 'Unrealism and Death in Contemporary Poetry'; discussion between Forrest-Thomson and Michel Couturier (with some interpolations by others), at Cambridge Poetry Festival, 18 April 1975, National Sound Archive T6023WR-7359W.

BIOGRAPHICAL AND CRITICAL STUDIES

Armstrong, Isobel, 'Feeling and Playing', *Adam International Review*, 391–3 (1975), 50–1.

Fraser, G. S., 'Veronica: A Tribute', *Adam International Review*, 391–3 (1975), 43–5.

Gregson, Ian, 'A Various Art: Veronica Forrest-Thomson and Denise Riley', *Contemporary Poetry and Postmodernism: Dialogue and Estrangement* (Basingstoke: Macmillan, 1996), 192–208.

Harrison, Martin, 'An Introduction to Veronica Forrest-Thomson's Work', in Denise Riley (ed.), *Poets on Writing: Britain, 1970–1991* (Basingstoke: Macmillan, 1992), 216–21.

Keery, James, 'Blossoming Synechdoches: A Study of Veronica Forrest-Thomson', *Bête Noire*, 10/11 (1990/1991), 109–22.

——, 'A Unique Voice', *PN Review*, 17:4 (1991), 85–7.

Larrissy, Edward, 'Poets of *A Various Art*: J. H. Prynne, Veronica Forrest-Thomson, Andrew Crozier', in Romana Huk and James Acheson (eds), *Contemporary British Poetry: Essays in Theory and Criticism* (New York: State University of New York Press, 1996), 63–79.

Lawson, F. Q., 'The Outrageous Friend', *Adam International Review*, 391–3 (1975), 52–3.

London, John, 'Veronica Forrest-Thomson and the Art of Artifice', *fragmente*, 4 (1991), 80–8. Review of *Collected Poems and Translations*.

Mark, Alison, 'Hysteria and Poetic Language: A Reading of the Work of Veronica Forrest-Thomson', *Women: A Cultural Review*, 5:3 (1994), 264–77.

——, 'Reading Between the Lines: Identity and the Early Poems of Veronica Forrest-Thomson', in *Kicking Daffodils: Essays on Twentieth-Century Women Poets* (Edinburgh: Edinburgh University Press, 1996), 210–26.

——, 'Veronica Forrest-Thomson: Towards a Linguistically Investigative Poetics', *Poetics Today*, 20:4 (1999), 645–61.

143

————, 'Poetic Relations and Related Poetics: Veronica Forrest-Thomson and Charles Bernstein', in Romana Huk (ed.), *Assembling Alternatives* (Hanover, NH: Wesleyan University Press, forthcoming).

McHale, Brian, 'Making (Non)sense of Postmodernist Poetry', in Michael Toolan (ed.), *Language, Text and Context: Essays in Stylistics* (London: Routledge, 1992), 6–36.

McKie, Michael, 'Ashbery or Lowell?', *English* (1982), 162–8. Review of *Poetic Artifice*.

Morgan, Edwin, review of *Identi-kit*, *Tlaloc*, 15 (13 July 1967).

Perril, Simon, 'Contemporary British Poetry and Modernist Invention' (unpublished PhD thesis, Cambridge, 1995). One chapter on Forrest-Thomson, concentrating on *On the Periphery*.

Porter, Peter, review of *On the Periphery*, *Observer*, 12 December 1976.

————, 'On the Best Battlefields No Dead Bodies', *Observer*, 5 August 1990. Review of *Collected Poems and Translations*.

Raitt, Suzanne, 'Veronica Forrest-Thomson *Collected Poems and Translations*', *Women: A Cultural Review*, 1:3 (1990), 304–8.

Smith, Paul (ed.), 'Trajectory Harm', *Spindrift*, 1 [1977?], review section, last two pages: discusses *On the Periphery*.

LANGUAGE WRITING

Andrews, Bruce, and Charles Bernstein (eds), *The L=A=N=G=U=A=G=E Book* (Carbondale and Edwardsville: Southern Illinois University Press, 1984).

Bartlett, Lee, 'What is "Language Poetry"?', *Critical Inquiry*, 12 (Summer 1986), 741–52.

Bernstein, Charles, *Artifice of Absorption* (Philadelphia: Singing Horse Press/Paper Air, 1987).

————, *A Poetics* (Cambridge, MA: Harvard University Press, 1992).

————, (ed.), *The Politics of Poetic Form: Poetry and Public Policy* (New York: Roof, 1990).

fragmente, 2 (Autumn 1990).

Hartley, George, *Textual Politics and the Language Poets* (Bloomington: Indiana University Press, 1989).

Hejinian, Lyn, *Writing as an Aid to Memory* (Berkeley: The Figures, 1978/ Los Angeles: Sun & Moon Press, 1996).

————, *My Life* (Los Angeles: Sun & Moon Press, 1987).

Howe, Susan, *The Europe of Trusts* (Los Angeles: Sun & Moon Press, 1990).

————, *Frame Structures: Early Poems 1974–1979* (New York: New Directions, 1996).

Mengham, Rod, review of five Language texts, *Textual Practice*, 3:1

(1989), 115–24.

Messerli, Douglas (ed.), *'Language' Poetries: An Anthology* (New York: New Directions, 1987).

Morgan, Edwin, *Language, Poetry and Language Poetry*, The Kenneth Allott Lectures, No. 5 (Liverpool: Liverpool Classical Monthly, 1990).

O'Sullivan, Maggie (ed.), *Out of Everywhere: Linguistically Innovative Poetry by Women in North America & the UK* (London: Reality Street Editions, 1996).

Perelman, Bob (ed.), *Talks, Hills* 6/7 (Spring 1980).

——, (ed.), *Writing/Talks* (Carbondale: Southern Illinois University Press, 1985).

——, *The Marginalization of Poetry: Language Writing and Literary History* (Princeton: Princeton University Press, 1996).

Perloff, Marjorie, *The Poetics of Inderminacy: Rimbaud to Cage* (Princeton: Princeton University Press, 1981). Reprints 'The Word as Such: L=A=N=G=U=A=G=E poetry in the eighties'.

——, ' "The sweet taste of artichokes, the lobes of autobiography": Lyn Hejinian's *My Life*', *fragmente*, 2 (1990), 49–56.

——, *Radical Artifice: Writing Poetry in the Age of Media* (Chicago: University of Chicago Press, 1991).

——, *Wittgenstein's Ladder: Poetic Language and the Strangeness of the Ordinary* (Chicago: University of Chicago Press, 1996).

Reinfeld, Linda, *Language Poetry: Writing as Rescue* (Baton Rouge: Louisiana State University Press, 1992).

Sheppard, Robert, 'Elsewhere and Everywhere: Other New (British) Poetries', *Critical Survey*, 10:1 (1998), 17–32.

——, *Far Language: Poetics and Linguistically Innovative Poetry 1978–1997* (Exeter: Stride, 1999).

Shetley, Vernon, 'The Return of the Repressed: Language Poetry and the New Formalism', *After the Death of Poetry: Poet and Audience in Contemporary America* (Durham, NC: Duke University Press, 1993), 135–64.

Silliman, Ron, *The New Sentence* (New York: Roof Books, 1989).

——, (ed.), *In the American Tree* (Orono: National Poetry Federation, University of Maine at Orono, 1986).

Ward, Geoff, *Language Poetry and the American Avant-garde* (Keele: British Association for American Studies, 1993).

Watten, Barrett, *Total Syntax* (Carbondale and Edwardsville, IL: Southern Illinois University Press, 1985).

——, New Meaning and Poetic Vocabulary: From Coleridge to Jackson Mac Low', *Poetics Today*, 18:2 (1997), 147–86.

von Halberg, Robert (ed.), *Politics and Poetic Value* (Chicago: University of Chicago Press, 1987).

145

OTHER WORKS MENTIONED IN THE TEXT

Adcock, Fleur (ed.), *The Faber Book of 20th Century Women's Poetry* (London: Faber, 1987).

Armstrong, Isobel, *Victorian Poetry: Poetry, Poetics and Politics* (London: Routledge, 1993).

Baldick, Chris, *Concise Dictionary of Literary Terms* (Oxford: Oxford University Press, 1990).

Barthes, Roland, *Mythologies* (Paris: Seuil, 1957).

——, *Essais Critiques* (Paris: Seuil, 1964).

——, *S/Z* (Paris: Seuil, 1970).

——, *Critical Essays*, trans. Richard Howard (Evanston, IL: Northwestern University Press, 1972).

——, *S/Z*, trans. Richard Miller (New York: Hill and Wang, 1974).

——, *Image Music Text*, selected and trans. Stephen Heath (London: Fontana, 1977).

——, *Barthes: Selected Writings*, ed. Susan Sontag (London: Fontana, 1983).

——, *Writing Degree Zero & Elements of Semiology*, trans. Annette Lavers and Colin Smith (London: Cape, 1984).

——, *Mythologies*, selected and trans. Annette Lavers (London: Vintage, 1993).

Benvenuto, Bice, and Roger Kennedy, *The Works of Jacques Lacan: An Introduction* (London: Free Association Books, 1986).

Bloom, Harold, *The Anxiety of Influence: A Theory of Poetry* (London: Oxford University Press, 1973).

Chaucer, Geoffrey, *The Works*, ed. F. N. Robinson (London: Oxford University Press, 1957).

Cixous, Hélène, and Catherine Clément, *The Newly Born Woman*, trans. Betsy Wing (Manchester: Manchester University Press, 1986).

Coleridge, Samuel Taylor, *Biographia Literaria or Biographical Sketches of my Literary Life and Opinions* (London: Dent, 1956).

Culler, Jonathan, *Structuralist Poetics: Structuralism, Linguistics and the Study of Literature* (London: Routledge & Kegan Paul, 1975).

——, *The Pursuit of Signs* (London: Routledge & Kegan Paul, 1981).

——, *Barthes* (London: Fontana, 1990).

Dante Alighieri, *The Comedy of Dante Alighieri the Florentine, Cantica II: Purgatory*, trans. Dorothy L. Sayers (Harmondsworth: Penguin, 1955).

Daniel, Arnaut, *La Vita e le opere del trovatore Arnaldo Daniello*, ed. Ugo A. Canello (Halle: Niemeyer, 1883).

——, *Le Canzoni di Arnaut Daniel*, 2 vols, ed. Maurizio Perugi (Milan: Ricciardi, 1978).

Donne, John, *The Poems*, ed. H. J. C. Grierson (London: Oxford

University Press / Humphry Milford, 1929).

Eliot, T. S., *Collected Poems 1909–1962* (London: Faber and Faber, 1963).

——, *Selected Prose*, ed. Frank Kermode (London: Faber and Faber, 1975).

Empson, William, 'Donne and the Rhetorical Tradition', *Kenyon Review*, 11 (1949), 571–87.

——, 'Donne the Spaceman', *Kenyon Review*, 19 (1957), 337–99.

——, *Seven Types of Ambiguity* (London: Chatto and Windus, 1953).

——, *Collected Poems* (London: Chatto and Windus, 1955).

——, *Some Versions of Pastoral: A Study of the Pastoral Form in Literature* (Harmondsworth: Penguin, 1966).

——, *Argufying: Essays on Literature and Culture*, ed. John Haffenden (London: Hogarth Press, 1988).

Felman, Shoshana, 'To Open the Question', in *Literature and Psychoanalysis: The Question of Reading: Otherwise*, Yale French Studies 55/56 (1977), 5–10.

Freud, Sigmund, *Standard Edition of the Complete Psychological Works of Sigmund Freud*, trans. from the German under the general editorship of James Strachey; in collaboration with Anna Freud assisted by Alix Strachey and Alan Tyson, 24 vols (London: Tavistock Publications, 1955–74).

Genette, Gérard, *Figures of Literary Discourse*, trans. Alan Sheridan (Oxford: Blackwell, 1982).

Gombrich, Ernst, *Art and Illusion: A Study in the Psychology of Pictorial Representation* (New York: Pantheon, 1960).

Graves, Robert, *The Greek Myths*, vol. 1 (Harmondsworth: Penguin, 1957).

Haffenden, John, *Novelists in Interview* (London: Methuen, 1985).

Herrmann, Claudine, *Les Voleuses de langue* (Paris: Des Femmes, 1979).

Hutcheon, Linda, *A Theory of Parody: The Teachings of Twentieth-Century Art Forms* (London: Methuen, 1985).

——, *Irony's Edge: The Theory and Politics of Irony* (London: Routledge, 1994).

Keats, John, *The Letters*, 4th edn (London: Oxford University Press, 1952).

Kristeva, Julia, *Semiotiké: Recherches pour une sémanalyse* (Paris: Seuil, 1969).

——, *Desire in Language: A Semiotic Approach to Literature and Art*, ed. Leon S. Roudiez, trans. Thomas Gora, Alice Jardine, Leon S. Roudiez (Oxford: Blackwell, 1980).

——, *Revolution in Poetic Language*, trans. Margaret Waller (New York: Columbia University Press, 1984).

Lacan, Jacques, *Écrits: A Selection*, trans. Alan Sheridan (London: Tavistock, 1977).

147

Laplanche, J., and J.-B. Pontalis, *The Language of Psycho-Analysis*, trans. Donald Nicholson-Smith (London: Hogarth Press and the Institute of Psycho-Analysis, 1983).

Lavers, Annette, *Roland Barthes: Structuralism and After* (London: Methuen, 1982).

Lodge, David (ed.), *Modern Criticism and Theory* (Harlow: Longman, 1988).

MacLeish, Archibald, *New & Collected Poems 1917–1976* (Boston: Houghton Miflin, 1976).

Mann, Thomas, *Doctor Faustus: The Life of the German Composer Adrian Leverkühn as Told by a Friend* (London: Secker & Warburg, 1976).

Marlowe, Christopher, *The Jew of Malta*, ed. N. W. Bawcutt (Manchester: Manchester University Press, 1978).

Marvell, Andrew, *The Poems and Letters*, vol. 1, *Poems*, ed. H. M. Margoliouth (Oxford: Clarendon, 1927).

Nash, Cristopher, *World-Games: The Tradition of Anti-Realist Revolt* (London: Methuen, 1987).

Nicholls, Peter, *Modernisms: A Literary Guide* (Basingstoke: Macmillan, 1995).

Olson, Charles, *Selected Writings*, ed. Robert Creeley (New York: New Directions, 1950).

Pears, David, *Wittgenstein* (London: Fontana, 1985).

Perloff, Marjorie, *The Dance of the Intellect: Studies in the Poetry of the Pound Tradition* (Cambridge: Cambridge University Press, 1985).

Pound, Ezra, *Translations* (Norfolk, CT: New Directions, 1963).

——, *Literary Essays*, ed. T. S. Eliot (London: Faber and Faber, 1954).

Roberts, Philip Davies, *How Poetry Works: The Elements of English Poetry* (Harmondsworth: Penguin, 1986).

Quartermain, Peter, *Disjunctive Poetics: From Gertrude Stein and Louis Zukovsky to Susan Howe* (Cambridge: Cambridge University Press, 1992).

Sappho, *Sappho and the Greek Lyric Poets*, ed. Willis Barnstone (New York: Schocken, 1972).

Selden, Raman, *A Reader's Guide to Contemporary Literary Theory* (Hemel Hempstead: Harvester Wheatsheaf, 1985).

Sellar, W. C., and R. J. Yeatman, *1066 and All That, a Memorable History of England, Comprising All the Parts You Can Remember, Including 103 Good Things, 5 Bad Things, and 2 Genuine Dates* (Harmondsworth: Penguin/ Methuen, 1960).

Shakespeare, William, *King Richard II*, The Arden Shakespeare (London: Methuen, 1961).

——, *The Tempest*, The Arden Shakespeare (London: Methuen, 1964).

Shelley, Percy Bysshe, *Literary and Philosophical Criticism*, ed. John Shawcross (London: Frowde, 1909).

Shklovsky, Victor, 'Art as Technique', in Lee T. Lemon and Marion J. Reis (eds), *Russian Formalist Criticism: Four Essays* (Lincoln: University of Nebraska Press, 1965), 3–24.

Stein, Gertrude, *Look at Me Now and Here I am: Writings and Lectures 1909–45*, ed. Patricia Meyerowitz (Harmondsworth: Penguin, 1990).

Stevens, Wallace, *The Collected Poems* (London: Faber and Faber, 1984).

Todorov, Tzvetan, *Introduction to Poetics*, trans. Richard Howard (Minneapolis: University of Minnesota Press, 1981).

Wilhelm, James J., *Il Miglior Fabbro: The Cult of the Difficult in Daniel, Dante and Pound* (Orono: The National Poetry Foundation, University of Maine at Orono, 1982).

Wittgenstein, Ludwig, *Tractatus Logico-Philosophicus*, trans. C. K. Ogden (London: Routledge & Kegan Paul, 1985).

——, *Philosophical Investigations*, trans. G. E. M. Anscombe (Oxford: Blackwell, 1989).

——, *Zettel*, ed. G. E. M. Anscombe and G. H. von Wright, trans. G. E. M. Anscombe (Oxford: Blackwell, 1990).

Yeats, W. B., *The Poems: A New Edition*, ed. Richard R. Finneran (London: Macmillan, 1984).

Index

WRITERS AND THEIR WORK

RECENT & FORTHCOMING TITLES

Title	Author
Peter Ackroyd	*Susana Onega*
Kingsley Amis	*Richard Bradford*
Anglo-Saxon Verse	*Graham Holderness*
Antony and Cleopatra	*Ken Parker*
As You Like It	*Penny Gay*
W. H. Auden	*Stan Smith*
Alan Ayckbourn	*Michael Holt*
J. G. Ballard	*Michel Delville*
Djuna Barnes	*Deborah Parsons*
Aphra Behn 2/e	*Sue Wiseman*
John Betjeman	*Dennis Brown*
Edward Bond	*Michael Mangan*
Anne Brontë	*Betty Jay*
Emily Brontë	*Stevie Davies*
A. S. Byatt	*Richard Todd*
Byron	*Drummond Bone*
Caroline Drama	*Julie Sanders*
Angela Carter	*Lorna Sage*
Geoffrey Chaucer	*Steve Ellis*
Children's Literature	*Kimberley Reynolds*
Caryl Churchill 2/e	*Elaine Aston*
John Clare	*John Lucas*
S. T. Coleridge	*Stephen Bygrave*
Joseph Conrad	*Cedric Watts*
Crime Fiction	*Martin Priestman*
Shashi Deshpande	*Armrita Bhalla*
Charles Dickens	*Rod Mengham*
John Donne	*Stevie Davies*
Carol Ann Duffy 2/e	*Deryn Rees Jones*
Early Modern Sonneteers	*Michael Spiller*
George Eliot	*Josephine McDonagh*
English Translators of Homer	*Simeon Underwood*
Henry Fielding	*Jenny Uglow*
Veronica Forrest-Thomson – Language Poetry	*Alison Mark*
E. M. Forster	*Nicholas Royle*
Elizabeth Gaskell	*Kate Flint*
The *Gawain*-Poet	*John Burrow*
The Georgian Poets	*Rennie Parker*
William Golding	*Kevin McCarron*
Graham Greene	*Peter Mudford*
Ivor Gurney	*John Lucas*
Hamlet	*Ann Thompson & Neil Taylor*
Thomas Hardy	*Peter Widdowson*
David Hare	*Jeremy Ridgman*
Tony Harrison	*Joe Kelleher*
William Hazlitt	*J. B. Priestley; R. L. Brett (intro. by Michael Foot)*
Seamus Heaney 2/e	*Andrew Murphy*
George Herbert	*T.S. Eliot (intro. by Peter Porter)*
Henrik Ibsen	*Sally Ledger*

RECENT & FORTHCOMING TITLES

Title	Author
Kazuo Ishiguro	*Cynthia Wong*
Henry James – The Later Writing	*Barbara Hardy*
James Joyce	*Steven Connor*
Julius Caesar	*Mary Hamer*
Franz Kafka	*Michael Wood*
Hanif Kureishi	*Ruvani Ranasinha*
William Langland: *Piers Plowman*	*Claire Marshall*
King Lear	*Terence Hawkes*
Philip Larkin	*Laurence Lerner*
D. H. Lawrence	*Linda Ruth Williams*
Doris Lessing	*Elizabeth Maslen*
C. S. Lewis	*William Gray*
David Lodge	*Bernard Bergonzi*
Christopher Marlowe	*Thomas Healy*
Andrew Marvell	*Annabel Patterson*
Ian McEwan	*Kiernan Ryan*
Measure for Measure	*Kate Chedgzoy*
A Midsummer Night's Dream	*Helen Hackett*
Vladimir Nabokov	*Neil Cornwell*
V. S. Naipaul	*Suman Gupta*
Walter Pater	*Laurel Brake*
Brian Patten	*Linda Cookson*
Harold Pinter	*Mark Batty*
Sylvia Plath	*Elisabeth Bronfen*
Jean Rhys	*Helen Carr*
Richard II	*Margaret Healy*
Richard III	*Edward Burns*
Dorothy Richardson	*Carol Watts*
John Wilmot, Earl of Rochester	*Germaine Greer*
Romeo and Juliet	*Sasha Roberts*
Christina Rossetti	*Kathryn Burlinson*
Salman Rushdie	*Damian Grant*
Paul Scott	*Jacqueline Banerjee*
The Sensation Novel	*Lyn Pykett*
P. B. Shelley	*Paul Hamilton*
Wole Soyinka	*Mpalive Msiska*
Muriel Spark	*Brian Cheyette*
Edmund Spenser	*Colin Burrow*
Laurence Sterne	*Manfred Pfister*
J. R. R. Tolkien	*Charles Moseley*
Leo Tolstoy	*John Bayley*
Charles Tomlinson	*Tim Clark*
Anthony Trollope	*Andrew Sanders*
Victorian Quest Romance	*Robert Fraser*
Edith Wharton	*Janet Beer*
Angus Wilson	*Peter Conradi*
Mary Wollstonecraft	*Jane Moore*
Women's Gothic	*Emma Clery*
Virginia Woolf 2/e	*Laura Marcus*
Working Class Fiction	*Ian Haywood*
W. B. Yeats	*Edward Larrissy*
Charlotte Yonge	*Alethea Hayter*

TITLES IN PREPARATION

Title	Author
Chinua Achebe	*Nahem Yousaf*
Ama Ata Aidoo	*Nana Wilson-Tagoe*
Matthew Arnold	*Kate Campbell*
Margaret Atwood	*Marion Wynne-Davies*
Jane Austen	*Robert Miles*
John Banville	*Peter Dempsey*
Pat Barker	*Sharon Monteith*
Julian Barnes	*Matthew Pateman*
Samuel Beckett	*Keir Elam*
William Blake	*Steven Vine*
Elizabeth Bowen	*Maud Ellmann*
John Bunyan	*Tamsin Spargoe*
Cymbeline	*Peter Swaab*
Daniel Defoe	*Jim Rigney*
Anita Desai	*Elaine Ho*
Margaret Drabble	*Glenda Leeming*
John Dryden	*David Hopkins*
T. S. Eliot	*Colin MacCabe*
John Fowles	*William Stephenson*
Brian Friel	*Geraldine Higgins*
Athol Fugard	*Dennis Walder*
Nadine Gordimer	*Lewis Nkosi*
Geoffrey Grigson	*R. M. Healey*
Geoffrey Hill	*Andrew Roberts*
Gerard Manley Hopkins	*Daniel Brown*
Ted Hughes	*Susan Bassnett*
Samuel Johnson	*Liz Bellamy*
Ben Jonson	*Anthony Johnson*
John Keats	*Kelvin Everest*
Rudyard Kipling	*Jan Montefiore*
Charles and Mary Lamb	*Michael Baron*
Wyndham Lewis	*Andrzej Gasiorek*
Malcolm Lowry	*Hugh Stevens*
Macbeth	*Kate McCluskie*
Katherine Mansfield	*Andrew Bennett*
The Merchant of Venice	*Warren Chernaik*
John Milton	*Jonathan Sawday*
Bharati Mukherjee	*Manju Sampat*
Alice Munro	*Ailsa Cox*
R. K. Narayan	*Shirley Chew*
New Women Novelists of the Late 19th Century	*Gail Cunningham*
Grace Nichols	*Sarah Lawson-Welsh*
Edna O'Brien	*Amanda Greenwood*
Ben Okri	*Robert Fraser*
Caryl Phillips	*Helen Thomas*
Dennis Potter	*Derek Paget*
Religious Poets of the 17th Century	*Helen Wilcox*
Revenge Tragedy	*Janet Clare*
Samuel Richardson	*David Deeming*
Nayantara Sahgal	*Ranjana Ash*
Sir Walter Scott	*Harriet Harvey-Wood*
Mary Shelley	*Catherine Sharrock*

TITLES IN PREPARATION

Title	Author
Stevie Smith	*Martin Gray*
R. L. Stevenson	*David Robb*
Gertrude Stein	*Nicola Shaughnessy*
Bram Stoker	*Andrew Maunder*
Tom Stoppard	*Nicholas Cadden*
Jonathan Swift	*Ian Higgins*
Algernon Swinburne	*Catherine Maxwell*
The Tempest	*Gordon McMullan*
Tennyson	*Seamus Perry*
W. M. Thackeray	*Richard Salmon*
Three Avant-Garde Poets	*Peter Middleton*
Derek Walcott	*Stephen Regan*
Marina Warner	*Laurence Coupe*
Jeanette Winterson	*Margaret Reynolds*
Women Romantic Poets	*Anne Janowitz*
Women Writers at the Fin de Siècle	*Angelique Richardson*
Women Writers of the 17th Century	*Ramona Wray*